ACKNOWLEDGMENT

I would like to thank my Mother who kept pushing for this book to be done. I would also like to thank my children; Michelle, Monica and Michael. I hope this atones for all the missed birthday parties, Christmas days, and other holidays and family get-togethers, and all the weekend baseball and soccer games I never attended. I thought it was more important to be at work than to be at home. And to my wife of 48 years, Heleen, who suffered more than anyone. Whatever small success I have become I owe to her.

Special thanks go to the following who helped with the memory lapses and who kept repeating; "Yeah, but what about the time you did…" Bill Barnes, Gary Wiegand, Mike Moorhead, Stan Mowre, and of course, Bob Yerbury. If it wasn't for him I would have had a much more successful career, but not nearly as many stories. Bob was also a huge help in researching the stories. He kept every single piece of paper with a story that involved us.

I would like to thank Ron Corbin, Gary Kissinger, John Flammang, and Mick Martinesi for their assistance in editing the book.

Ernie Misner, long time friend and fellow hellion from high school, was a huge help in getting the cover done and for attempting to clear up some of the pictures I kept from the "day." If you want to see some quality photographic work, go to flickr.com/photos/erniemisner. He is truly talented.

Cover photo: Ernie Misner, owner, Guiding Light Photography, Lakewood, WA.

The events depicted in the book are as I remember them. It's been forty plus years since some occurred. If you disagree with anything, contact me.

Contents

YOU NEVER GET OUT ALIVE

I was floating above the bed and looked down at myself. I saw that I was surrounded by a white fog or cloud. In the middle of all of this was a pathway or tunnel. I was moving toward a lighter area that was almost glowing. I had no idea where I was going, but it was very quiet and peaceful. I have been here before I thought. I just can't remember the circumstances. I needed time to figure this out. Before I can come to any realization, I felt as if I have been kicked in the chest by a horse. All the peace and tranquility are gone and I am no longer moving toward the brightness. Now I am back in reality and find myself lying in a hospital bed, several people are hovering over me, and my chest feels like it is on fire. The person to my right is holding some kind of pad in each hand, and wires are coming out of the bottom of each one. Then I saw a needle descending; I got a shot and went back to sleep.

When I awoke I found my wife, Heleen, staring down at me. Now I remembered. I'm in the hospital.
I asked, "What's going on?"
She replied, "You died. They had to use electrical shocks to

get your heart started again."
"Oh! Is that all?" I drifted back to sleep.

I had been in Korea for the last month, and had just gotten back to the U.S. where I worked full time as a homicide detective for the Tacoma Police Department. When I'm not investigating assaults and murders, I spend time as a Special Agent for the Department of Defense. I had recently taken about twenty agents to Korea so they could assist the U.S Army Criminal Investigators. This was my eighth trip to Korea and it would be my last. There was a yearly exercise that saw an influx of active and reserve military into that country for war games. With that many soldiers coming into the country there was always an increase in crime. I spread agents all over South Korea to investigate Fraud, Diversions of Property, Sex Crimes, Assaults and other crimes. All of the agents were there for two weeks, except me. I had been in country for over a month. I went early to prepare for the arrival of the agents, then I supervised them and made sure they had everything they needed such as weapons, clothing, pay, and a place to live. As half of them rotated home, I brought the other half into country and repeated my duties.

I had to supervise the agents and could only do this by running all over Korea visiting them. I was stressed out.

During this time I was smoking two to three packs of cigarettes a day, and washing the nicotine down with copious amounts of bourbon. I was a train wreck waiting to happen. On March 30, 1986 I finally realized that the chest pain that was spreading down my left arm might be a warning sign from God and that I needed to dial back my life style. At that point in my existence, I was forty years old, had spent two tours of combat in Vietnam as a helicopter pilot, and had been a cop for seventeen years. I was working anywhere from three to four extra jobs and trying to start a business. I may have been an overachiever, or just a glutton for punishment. At any rate, I crumpled my last pack of cigarettes and with my lighter, threw the whole mess into a garbage can. Maybe it was not too late, I thought.

On April 2nd, I was home from Korea and back at work in homicide. I came home from work and my son and two nephews were playing basketball in the front driveway of our house. I shucked my coat and gun and joined the three of them. About fifteen minutes into this insanity, I felt like an elephant was sitting on my chest. I quit playing and went into the house to lie down. I was sweaty and decided to take a hot shower before crawling into bed. Let's see. I think the rules are; if you suspect you are having a heart attack - don't lie down; don't take a shower; don't ignore the symptoms, and seek immediate help. There may be five rules, but I only remembered to violate four of them.

After lying down for an hour, I had Heleen call the hospital and tell them I may be having a heart attack. They suggested an ambulance or Heleen could drive me to the emergency room. What Heleen heard was: "Load him in the car at your leisure. Drive slowly. Stop and pick up something for dinner and return the VHS tape. Maybe gas up the car."
I may have made that part up. It just seemed like the longest ride in history.

We finally arrived at Good Samaritan Hospital in Puyallup. I walked into the emergency room and the attending nurse took one look and stuck me on a gurney. A doctor came in and gave me a couple of shots. One of which was morphine to ease the pain. Then I was informed that I had had a heart attack and I was going to be put into the ICU. I was there for an hour or so and Heleen was on the phone in the hallway calling the police department and our family.

"Code Blue."
Everyone went running by Heleen and into my room. She dropped the phone and followed. Then she began yelling: "Do not resuscitate!" She thought I had more money than I really did or this was the chance to clear the garage of all the junked cars I kept dragging home. They paid her no attention. She kept waving what she claimed was a signed DNR statement from me. I think it might have been a grocery list. Luckily there was a medic from the fire department standing by my room; hitting on a nurse. When I flat lined and the alarm went off, he jumped on me and smacked my chest. This caused three ribs to crack and I was going to need more morphine for that pain. Then the doctor arrived and cranked up the defibrillator. He used it twice before getting a heartbeat and I ended up with a couple of nice round burn marks on my chest.

Now I got my ambulance ride! They didn't have an ICU at Good Sam that had enough staff and equipment to take care of me, so I was transferred to Tacoma General Hospital. I spent the next two weeks in intensive care before I was allowed to go home. I was on oxygen, morphine drip, fluids, restrictive diet, and God knows what else. My family helped by going to Frisco Freeze , a great little drive-in on Division Ave. They ate burgers and fries then would come in and kiss me. I could smell that food and taste it on their lips. If I would have had any strength, I would have strangled them.

I lay around the house for the next couple of months coming to terms with my mortality. I've had numerous close calls and several near death experiences as a combat helicopter pilot. On a couple of occasions I had seen my life flash before my eyes. Then I joined the cops with death and scary shit on a regular basis for seventeen more years. High speed chases, confrontations with armed individuals who only want to kill you, fights, dead bodies of all ages, going into houses and apartments undercover and buying drugs hoping your backup is paying attention, or that you even had backup.

I firmly believed that I had a life cup. Everyone has one and when it gets full your life ends. When I was a kid I started filling that cup with incidents that could and should have led to my demise. I was always racing fast cars and driving crazy. I had my share of beers as a kid and drove anyway. I skied the glaciers on Mt. Rainier, I went skin diving in the Puget Sound, and I joined the Army and was shipped off to war. More than once I was shot at or shot down, and I always marveled at my good fortune. I continued all through life putting more drops in the cup. The cup was maybe almost full, only I didn't know just how full. Would it be one more drop or did I have many more drops of space left. When it spilled over that was the end. Now it seemed to be leaking a tad. Or maybe I was just shaking a bit and causing it to slosh.

I had to return to work. My sick leave time was up. They wouldn't keep my spot open in homicide forever. Crime didn't stop and someone was needed to respond to those scenes. My desk was assigned to someone else and I was transferred to Crimes Against Property which dealt with burglaries, thefts, and non violent crimes. No one said anything to me, but maybe they were trying to do me a favor and reduce my stress levels. The same thing happened when I was undercover buying drugs. You get to the point where reality starts to blur. You are out on the imaginary limb and sawing it off with both hands. Someone else has to look at your behavior and decide you have had enough. You won't do it on your own.

I was back trying to find missing garbage can lids and other minor crimes. I hated it. After a life of adrenaline fixes, I'm sitting on my ass most of the time trying to figure out who stole what from whom. Boring!

I had more chest pains, not quite to the elephant level, and was taking about thirty different pills a day. I carried a bottle of nitroglycerine and found I needed to pop one of those on occasion. I went back to my cardiologist and after more tests, I was told that the heart damage was permanent and that I had lost 1/3 of my heart muscle. He informed me it was only a question of time before I had another heart attack or I would need heart bypass surgery.

I petitioned the pension board and was granted a medical retirement for the heart problems. I quietly turned in all my equipment and left without saying anything to anyone. The chief didn't kiss me goodbye, and I got no mementos for my service to the city.

MAYBERRY WITH A CAPITAL "F"

I was speeding down Main St. in a 68 Chevy Biscayne with the roof rack lights on, and the siren making its feeble noise. My partner was giving me directions because I had no idea where to go. It was February 1970 and I had been a policeman for a total of two days. Thirty days prior to that I was flying helicopters in Vietnam.

The fire dispatcher called us and said there was a report of a fight in an alley between at least two people and maybe more. We are the only cops on duty in this small city, and the dispatcher said he would call the next town closest to us and ask for backup. If we were lucky that means a couple of more cops may or may not show up. We didn't get lucky. They had their own town to worry about, and unless we declare an emergency they probably would not be coming. We can also call the Pierce County Sheriff's Office, but they are spread thin. Pierce County is the largest county in the State of Washington, area wise, but is undermanned. Most police departments have two officers working together at night. The PCSO is lucky to have two deputies working in the same twenty square mile box.

By following my partner's directions, I found myself sliding into an alley in a residential area of town. There are small houses sitting side-by-side with small yards, and detached garages. This town has not changed much from when it was incorporated in the 1890's. Farmers, some light industry, a car dealership or two, and the normal service companies of a small town. The city covers fewer than seven square miles, and has a population of about 4400 people. The people are predominately white middle class American, with a smattering of Indians. Tonight we get the Indians.

I arrived behind a cluster of single story duplexes which had seen better days. They were stylish when they were built in the late '40s, but have now become home to welfare recipients, and the out of work. These Indians fit both categories, so they were living here also. The Indians in our town spend all their waking hours getting drunk on the cheapest alcohol they can find. Fortified wine is their drink of choice. I believe they think that because it is fruit based that at least they are getting some nutrients. The real reason is that it is a dollar and change for a fifth.

My partner and I found four Indians in a small yard between two of the duplex units. Two women are standing over a body, and the fourth person is leaning against the side of the building. It was pitch black where we were and we were using the car's headlights to illuminate the area. I got out of the car and pulled my flashlight from the map pouch on the door. I walked over to the two women and shine my light down on the body at their feet. I have never seen a person so beat up in my entire life. I spent two tours in Vietnam and saw my share of dead people, but this guy takes the prize. What should have been a head is so grossly misshapen, it is all but unrecognizable. It was swollen to at least twice its normal size, and I can't tell if I am looking at the front or back. I think I'm looking at the eyes, but then I realize it could be the ears. There is just no way to tell. I also know the human body holds about five quarts of blood. There is at least two times that amount pooled around this guy's head.

I may be a brand new police officer, but I know a murder when I see one. I grabbed the Indian leaning against the wall, and asked him if he did this. He is drunk but coherent and said, "Yeah. I did it. He had it coming. He stole my wine."

I handcuffed the suspect and put him into the back seat of the police car. Meanwhile my partner has called for an ambulance, and is checking out the body. He is kneeling down next to the dead Indian when all of sudden he stands up and says, "Oh Shit. It's just Knobby. He gets beat up and looks like this all of the time." A few seconds later a large blood bubble comes popping out of what may be the mouth, and we can hear Knobby sucking air in and out.

Knobby went to Good Samaritan Hospital and lived to get beaten up again and again. His assailant went to our tiny little jail. He would remain there for the next couple of weeks eating on the city budget. Then he would be told to go and sin no more; the jail needed the space.

CIRCLE THE WAGONS AND THE IDIOTS

In January 1970, I was flying CH-47 Chinooks, around the jungles and mountains of South Vietnam. By February of that same year I had become a cop. I am not sure just how this happened. When I was in the Army I went to college at night and studied criminal justice. I thought that I needed a job flying. The only things I knew how to do were pilot helicopters and kill stuff. I looked around and found out that the Los Angeles Police Department had helicopters and they offered me a job when I finished my obligation to the Army. In 1968, I flew a helicopter out to Stockton, California, and had a chance to take a look at L.A. I have never seen so many people. There was so much concrete and highway, congestion and smog. It changed my perspective on where I might want to work, but I was still smitten with the whole cop thing.

When I got back from Vietnam, I started looking in my own backyard in Washington for a job as a policeman, and I still wanted to fly. Seattle had a couple of helicopters at this time, so I drove up there and submitted an application. I was informed that they were not currently giving tests for the recruit academy, but would give me a call in a few months when things opened up.

I contacted every police department in the state and was pretty much told the same thing. None of the large cities and counties had helicopters, and as much as they would like to have one, they couldn't afford one. The U.S. Government was giving surplus helicopters away, but the maintenance costs were outrageous. Vietnam vets were returning to the work force and most police departments were full. Then I noticed an ad in the local paper. A small town in Pierce County was looking to hire a police officer. Applications were now being accepted and a test would be administered. I knew I needed a job. I had a wife and two kids to support and had absolutely no prospects. I figured to get hired by some small hick department and then when it was time I would move to a large city and fly helicopters for them.

I reported to city hall and filled out the required application, and then waited. Within a week I was contacted by mail and told to report on the next Saturday for the written examination. This was to be conducted in the city council chambers. If I passed the written exam, then I would be called for a physical test. I showed up at the appointed time and place and was told the test was moved to the high school. Because of the large number of people wanting the job, the test had to be moved to a bigger building. When I got to the gymnasium there were over 200 men waiting. This was a standardized test to check your knowledge of math, English, reasoning skills, and general subjects. I finished the test in what seemed like a record time, and was one of the first to leave the building. When I got back outside, I immediately felt I had failed. I should have taken longer. Or I should have studied the questions and answers closer. I felt that I had hurried through it and should have used all of the allotted time.

I went home and whined about it for a couple of days until I got a call telling me I had passed. If I was still interested, I was to report to the high school athletic field on the following Saturday for the physical portion of the application. I showed up and was met with about fifty other guys who had scored well on the written portion. I had to do push-ups and sit-ups. I had to do chin-ups and weight lifting. Then there was a timed one mile run. I aced everything. I had just spent eight months in Vietnam and was in excellent condition. I was a lean, mean killing machine. Plus I was only twenty-four years old, and very motivated to be employed.

I went back home and waited. A few days later I got another call. This call informed me that I had scored in the top ten on the written examination and had scored first on the physical test. I was asked to come out to the city council chambers on the following Monday evening and be interviewed by the chief of police and the mayor. I was excited to be employed and on my way to a flying career with some big department.

On that Monday, I went out to the town and spent about an hour talking to the city council about my time in Vietnam as a pilot. When I finished the oral interview, the chief said he had made his decision and, if I wanted the job, I was his new patrolman. Holy shit. I'm a cop. He asked how soon I could start and I told him I had nothing pressing and could work that night if I just had a gun and badge.

The next day was soon enough for him and I showed up

bright and early to get sworn in and get issued my equipment. There was a large closet with a bunch of uniform pants and shirts so I rummaged through these castoffs until I found a couple of outfits that would fit. Just as I did in the Army, I figured I would take the clothes to a tailor and have them adjusted. I learned early in my military career that image is everything, and if you look like a sad sack, you will be treated like one.

I was handed a gun belt, two bullet pouches, a handcuff case and handcuffs, and a sap. The sap is a leather case about nine inches long. Inside the leather are molded lead and a spring steel shank. On one end is a leather handle for your hand. The sap is designed to get a suspect’s attention. If he ignores you, and is not listening to the gentle instructions he is receiving, you place the sap gently across his collarbone, elbow, shins, or noggin, and ring his bell. This gets the individuals focus back where it belongs.

Next came the most important piece of equipment an officer can have: The gat. The heater. Your roscoe. The shootin' iron. The six gun. Your piece. I’m handed a Smith and Wesson with a six inch barrel, and it’s sitting in a swivel holster. I'm thinking the last guy to use this probably patrolled from horseback. I put the gun and holster on the gun belt and tried it on. The holster was hanging down about four inches below the belt and then the gun was hanging down even further. I looked like Barney Fife. This thing was dragging the ground and I was going to have to put a wheel on the end so it could follow me around.

The chief gave me six bullets to put in the gun and six more for the ammo pouch. I had a bad experience in Vietnam with not having enough bullets and so I asked for six more. I had crash landed in a rice paddy, and found myself fending off the suspected hordes with only six bullets. I wasn't making that mistake again. The chief said to me, "Good God. This is a small town. Who are you thinking of shooting?"
"Eighteen is my lucky number," I replied with a dead eye stare.

I am introduced to the sergeant, who we shall call Kyle. Kyle has been a cop for several years, first in a large city in the north, and now in a small town in the south. It's going to take me a couple of months before I find out that I have stumbled into "Peyton Place on Acid" thus the need to

attach pseudo names to this group of co-workers.
Kyle took me on a tour of the town which used up about one hour. We then parked on Main Street and walked in and out of all the business to meet the owners. This is small town America. The mayor runs one business. All the city council members have either a bar, pharmacy, car lot, or insurance agency. The mayor's family work for him or for a council member. The council member's families and friends all work with each other, and every single person knows every other single person. It only takes me about a half a day to realize there are two factions in town; those people who have the power and those wishing they did. I am told by town people that the chief and mayor are the most wonderful leaders in the free world, or that both of them should be taken out and shot.

It is day two and I am enrolled in the, "Small Town Police Training Academy". I am handed a map of the city and told to go to work.
"Call in if you have any questions."
This was pretty much all the police training I was going to get. I didn't have a clue. I started driving around town looking at everything and talking to whoever I met.

Everyone in town seemed nice and they answered all my questions about the city. I went back to the main street through the business district and parked. I then retraced my steps from the previous day and met again with all the owners. When it ,got dark I teamed up with Sergeant Kyle and got to meet the Indians.

Day three. Now we are talking action. I'm on the night shift working with another cop who I'll call 'Fats'. This guy is so overweight that he can barely fit in the police car. When I met him at the start of the shift, he was eating. At the end of the shift he was still stuffing the food in. I remember him having a motorcycle for a short time. It was a Harley and had the radio controls located on the dash above the gas tank. He sold the bike because every time he sat down he changed the channel or the volume on the radio.

We spent about an hour on our shift and he told me it's time to feed the inmates. I had no idea what he's talking about, but we headed back to the station and parked in the alley. I followed him inside to the two little jail cells we had and he unlocks both, yelling at the prisoners to get outside and into the car. The four of us then drive to a local restaurant and park in front. He herds the two of them inside and into a booth. They got served the daily special just like anyone else and no one is watching them to make sure they don't steal the silverware. Fats was too busy eating his own dinner to be worried about the two crooks. I finally asked what we were doing and Fats informs me that when we have guests in our jail, we take them out three times a day and bring them to the restaurant for their meals. We never have big time criminals; they'd get booked into the County Jail. We house the town drunks or someone serving time for traffic violations. By the time this night is over we will have one more for breakfast, after we make an arrest for Driving Under the Influence (DUI).

I spent the next few nights working either with Sgt. Kyle, Fats, or Dewey (Dewey is a phonetic saying for DUI) I'm starting to learn just what this police department is made of. Dewey had been arrested in his previous life for Driving Under the Influence thus the pseudonym 'Dewey'. He currently had no driver's license and had a conviction on his record. That didn't stop the chief from making him an officer. He just told Dewey not to get caught anywhere driving, and he would protect him while he was at work

inside the city limits.
Then there was Fats who due to his obesity could not get hired by any real police department. He was single and lived with his mother, and his days were spent going from meal to meal.

Another officer was Patrolman Hemingway. He picked up this moniker due to the fact that he could not write a report to save his life. He would respond to an incident at the start of the shift, or make an arrest and eight hours later he would still be trying to get the report written. If you were unlucky enough to encounter him in the station, you would end up sitting there and continually spelling words for him. It was easier just to write the report yourself. Hemingway was illiterate, and it was rumored that he had never finished high school. This didn't stop the chief from hiring him, and that was one more officer who owed his job to the boss.

This brings me back around to Kyle. He was intelligent, well trained by a larger police force, very outgoing and my first friend in the department. He was also another who owed his job to the chief. It seems Kyle had gotten caught sharing his favors with the wrong woman, at his previous job. He got fired and moved a few hundred miles away. The chief of course wanted to surround himself with men he could control, and what better way than to have them beholden to him for their very existence. Then I started hearing rumors from the other guys that Kyle spent almost all of his shifts at night, so that the chief can make visits to Kyle's wife. I was led to believe there was blackmail involved. The chief had told Kyle of course that he could fire him at any time. All he had to do is a background check with Kyle's previous employer. The chief had already done this, but did not disclose that fact to anyone. The chief had a little talk with Kyle's wife and told her that if her favors were to be had on occasion, then he wouldn't fire her husband.

Holy Shit! I thought I had seen everything there was to see in Vietnam, including a pink elephant. Now here I am right in the middle of more damn drama than I can handle, and I'm seeing thing I never dreamed.

INSTANT COP

There is really nothing much happening in this little town. We have the Friday and Saturday night fights in the bars. The reported thefts of garbage can lids. The usual bad check, and maybe a horse loose and walking the streets.

I was given a ticket book and a list of offenses, and it was left to my own judgment to write a ticket or issue a warning. When I was a kid, I got more than my share of speeding tickets, so I was pretty lenient on the kids around town. I usually only had to give them "The Look," and it was enough to stop whatever was going on. Once in a while I wrote them a citation, but always placed a big "W" on it which indicated that it was a warning. That way they did not have to pay a fine, but they knew there was a record of the ticket somewhere.

I thought I was doing fine until I got called in by the chief who informed me that I really needed to write more tickets. I was given a major street, which ran through town, as my assigned spot. This street was used by those living outside

the city to get from one side to the other on their way north to work in the big cities.
The chief explained, “They don’t live here, and they don’t vote here. They are fair game for revenue.”

I was assigned to work this street for two hours every morning and two hours every afternoon. I had an unmarked police car and was given a radar gun. I was shown how to turn it on and how to turn it off and, with that, I was sent on my way.

Now I’m really pissing people off. Not only am I stopping them to issue a ticket, but I am making them late for work. I finally realize that the best thing I can do is be a little more visible. So I started parking a wee bit more into the street. Hopefully they’ll see me and slow down before the radar picked them up. This worked for about half the people, and the other half were oblivious. So my next solution was to put my foot on the brake pedal. With the car parked out in the street a ways, and the back end lit up with brake lights, I figure I’m doing all that is possible to warn the drivers. When I was still stopping cars for speeding, I figured there was no dealing with the dumbest, so those drivers got the tickets. I was also getting the people who lived and worked in our town.

"Do you know who I am?"

"Do you know who my cousin is?"

"I used to babysit the mayor!"

"I used to be the mayor."

"Don't you eat in my café?"

There is just no way are you going to write a resident a ticket if you know what's good for you.

This duty went on for a while, but being a small town in a rural area, it didn't take long for everyone to figure out that there was a police car sitting in the same spot every day and he was writing tickets for speeding. All of the commuters switched to another road outside of town, and I was removed from the radar trap.

A few days later I was called into the office for Part II, of the "Small Town Police Academy." Sgt Kyle informed me that even though I spent the last five years in the U.S Army and had two tours of combat in Vietnam, I was sort of required to show I could shoot my service revolver. He grabbed a box of bullets and away we went to the city

owned water tower (aka the police shooting range). The tower was outside the city limits by a mile or so and sat in the trees on a hillside. We drove out and parked, and then set up a couple of targets against a dirt bank. I pulled my gun out and made sure it was loaded, and then commenced to aim at the first target. I pulled the trigger and nothing happened. I opened the cylinder and rechecked that I had real bullets in the gun.
"Yup! I have six bullets."

There is the trigger, hammer and firing pin. Let's try this again. I pulled back the hammer, took aim, and BAM! Well it worked that time. I then tried to squeeze a second shot off. The hammer went back and fell, but no round went off. We finally did some further checking and discovered that the cylinder was totally worn out. Instead of spinning and stopping with the next bullet under the hammer, the cylinder might be off by as much as a half a bullet. The firing pin was falling either on the cylinder or next to the primer on the bullet. Every once in a while everything would align and the gun would fire. Great! I have been carrying a gun which doesn't even work.

Back to the station we go and I get to trade in the ground dragging "Barney Special" for a gun with a shorter barrel and a nicer holster. This gun had been "Saved for a special occasion." I guess having a rookie with a gun that may or may not work, qualified as special. That ended all formal training for the new guy on the force. I was to become a cop by osmosis.

TEMPTATIONS

More than a singing group

After a couple of months on the force, I was on a semi-permanent swing shift with the occasional graveyard shift when Kyle was not around. The night shift was a hell of a lot more interesting than cruising around in the day time trying to find something to do. If it's going to happen, it will happen after the sun goes down. People lay around all day thinking up things they can do when it gets dark. But this was a small town, and small town rules apply. One person stopped for driving drunk will get a ride home and his car will be left for him to retrieve the next day. The next person will find his butt on the way to jail because he is on the chief's or mayor's shit list.

It is a Friday night around 10:00 pm. and I got a call regard a bar fight at Freddy's Freight Car. This is a local bar and restaurant, and coincidentally is where we feed our prisoners three times a day. I was the only police officer on duty, and the nearest backup is only who knows where. This is Friday and every police officer is busy. I told the dispatcher that I was on the way to the fight, and he told me to call back later so that he knows I'm alive.

Just like flying combat in Vietnam, I had to adapt and overcome. I pulled up in the alley because the bar was located in the rear of the building. The restaurant portion was out front. I got out of the police car and opened both rear doors. I then walked around the place and went in the front door. I sauntered over to the counter sat down, and ordered a cup of coffee. I told the waitress to go into the bar and tell whoever was fighting, to go out and get in the police car and I would be right along. She looked at me like I was nuts, but I sure as hell didn't want to go into the bar and tangle with a couple of guys. Sure as God made little green apples, two guys may be trying to kill each other, but as soon as a cop shows up, they will join sides and try and kill the cop. No one else is going to lend me a hand either. I have since spent thirty years in law enforcement, and I never remember hearing, "Hi Officer. I see you have your hands full with these eleven-teen assholes. Let me wrestle with a few of them for you."

I finished my coffee and walked back around the building, and sure as hell there they were, sitting in the back seat. Two young men with a little blood leaking from their noses and what looks like the start of a shiner or two. I asked them why they were fighting and who won, and neither had an answer. I then asked them why they decided to come out and sit in the police car. They both said that it was no use trying to hide or run away. Everybody in town knew them, and the judge would just get more pissed off if he had to issue a warrant for their arrest.

I went back into the bar and asked the bartender what the damages were. He said they had broken a couple of chairs, and a few glasses and the total was maybe $40 or $50. All the witnesses agreed it was a mutual fight over some perceived slight, and no one wanted to have to go to court.
"Okay. I admit it. Your girlfriend has more teeth than mine."
"Yup! But mine is fatter."
So I held court out in the alley. If they agreed to shake hands and pay the bar, everyone could be on their way.

I worked with Dewey one late afternoon. We were on swing shift but had just started for the day. He was driving in circles on one side of town and I was making continuous left turns on the other side. Dispatch called and said, "Go see the manager of the apartment building on Elm Street. She says one of her tenants won't answer his door and it stinks all over the hallway." I had no idea what this may mean but I headed over and met Dewey as he pulled up. Dewey told me to go on up to the listed apartment and he will go find the manager. I climbed the stairs to the second floor and walked about half way down the hallway when the odor hit me. Now I knew what dispatch meant by stink. Once you had smelled a dead body, you will always remember that smell. It is like the "burning shit barrels" in Vietnam. The troops crapped into a half of a fifty-five gallon barrel. These were lit on fire at the end of the day, using diesel fuel. That is how the waste was disposed of. There is no way to describe it to someone else, but you will never forget it.

Dewey was coming down the hall with this little shriveled up gnome who I swear is cackling. I keep hearing her telling Dewey, "He's dead. I just know he's dead." Cackle-Cackle-Cackle. When they get to the door of the apartment, Dewey asked her if she has a key, and she replies that she does. With that she unlocked the door. As it swung open, I saw a

man lying face down on the linoleum. Before Dewey and I can say anything or make a move, the gnome rushed in, grabbed the dead guy by the hair on the back of his head and lifts. The dead guy's face stuck to the floor, and the rest of his head came up, spilling maggots all over the vinyl.
"See. I told you he was dead." Cackle-Cackle-Cackle.

I exited stage left and just made it to the grass out front where I ruined the pretty shine on my police shoes. Then I had to stand around and wait for the medical examiner. It wasn't very comfortable with the puke sticking to my socks.

One of the guys was off sick, so I pulled a day shift on the weekend. The chief always worked the day shift Monday to Friday, usually with Hemmingway, and the rest of us got the nights and weekends. Dispatch called and said I had a call holding in the station from the military. Maybe I was being recalled because they needed more cannon fodder in Nam, or they finally decided to make me a general. Wherever you were in the city, it would take you about two minutes to get to the station, so I told dispatch to tell the caller, I would be right there.

I arrived back at our little office and picked up the phone. On the other end was the military police, and my first thought was what did I do, and how did they find out? The M.P. informed me that they were looking for an AWOL soldier who had a wife living in our town. They asked if I wasn't busy, would I go by and see if he was staying with her. If I found him, I could arrest him, and hold him for the military. I told them, "Well! Look here, guys. I'm really busy fighting crime, and trying to bring law and order to the huddled masses, but I'll see what I can do."

I immediately left the station and drove the three city blocks to the wife's listed address. I walked up to the front door and knocked and who should answer but the AWOL soldier I'm after. Just to be sure I asked him his name, and he confirmed that he was who I was looking for. I told him the military wanted him for being AWOL and he said he knew. I then asked, "Why are you AWOL?" He replied, "They keep restricting me to the base at Ft Lewis and I know I'm headed for Vietnam. I just want to be home on the weekends with my wife." This was now getting on to Sunday afternoon and he said he was ready to go back anyway.

I took him out and put him in the car and then the two of us drove back to the police department. I called the Military Police and they told me, “Damn! That was quick. We are coming your way so we’ll swing by and pick him up.”

An hour later two Military Policemen arrived and took the poor guy into custody. They then took down my name and address and told me I would be getting a check from Uncle Sam for $25.00. This was the current bounty on AWOL soldiers. I was making about $400.00 a month and they are giving me $25.00 for driving this G.I. to the station. Hallelujah! I began cruising every street in town, looking for guys with short haircuts.

My soldier took a liking to me and would go AWOL about every other weekend. When he did, he would find out what shift I was working. He would call me up and I would go “arrest” him. Then I would drive him to the M.P. station in Tacoma and collect my check.

Have I mentioned that there was not much to do in this little town? For excitement I would drive the police car out to a stretch of freeway that was located not far from town. At that time there were maybe two miles of concrete with a posted speed limit of 60 mph. I would start at one end and see how fast I could make that old Chevy go. Then I would turn around and go in the other direction, always trying to beat my last time. There wasn't much traffic out there anyway, but I would sit and wait for any cars to pass before I made my speed runs.

"Let's see. Two miles at 100 mph is about forty seconds. Turn around and do it again. Now the grand total is up to the neighborhood of one and a half minutes. Do this again later in the shift and we now have three minutes. Three minutes from eight hours of the shift, leaves seven hours and fifty-seven minutes of boredom."

I needed to find more things to do.

When the boredom got lifted, it really got lifted. I'm out on the edge of town at night all by myself. I spotted one of them hippy vans driving down the street, and I just knew they were up to no good. At the very least, they were probably smoking the devil weed. I got behind the van and then turned on the roof lights and pulled the VW over. I walked up to the driver's side, and the window started rolling down.

Inside on the driver's side is this gorgeous little blonde wearing a see through set of baby doll pajamas. Sitting in the passenger seat is an equally cute girl who is similarly dressed. My boredom began to lift.

I was standing there trying to act cool, and not stare at these two half naked chicks. They grabbed their purses and hopped out of the van to show me their I.D. I also got to see everything else they possessed, and everything was looking fine. I asked them where they are headed and they responded, "All of us are going to San Francisco to join in the love movement."

Or they could have said, "We are going to Mars and start a colony."

I wasn't paying a whole lot of attention to the dialog. I did catch the part about "all," and asked if anyone else was in the van. The two replied: "Yes. Missy is in back."
They then pounded on the side of the van, and Missy popped out, wearing the requisite see through jammies. Now I had three cuties and I'm definitely outnumbered. Should I go down fighting, or just surrender? This is when I was asked the one question that has lingered in my mind for the last

forty-two years, “Officer. Why don’t you jump in the van and go with us to San Francisco?”

All I had to do was hang my gun belt on the rear view mirror, call dispatch, and tell them where they could find the police car. I could spend the drive time to California letting my hair grow long, and I could learn how to smoke dope. Nah!

Plus I had a loving wife at home who I would sorely miss, and she would track-me-down and cut off my nuts.

A CROOK BY ANY OTHER NAME

I was spending more and more time with Kyle, who didn't seem to have a friend anywhere around. He had confided in me about his wife and the chief, and a lot of other things that have been going on. The chief handles all the big crimes in the town. These are mainly bad checks that someone has written to one of the town's businesses. If you are a friend of the chief's then your case got handled. On the other hand, if you don't get along with the chief your case will never see the light of day.

The same goes for parking violations. There is "No Parking" signs posted, but if you own the business right there and you need to park, and you are on a first name basis with the chief then go ahead and park. No problem! If you are not buddies, then expect a ticket or the tow truck will make an appearance.

The chief had called most of the officers into his office, and told us to stay out of certain businesses. We had one older gentleman who had worked for the city, and had retired. He then opened up his own little drive-in restaurant inside the city limits. There were only so many places a cop could eat at night. Because he didn't get along with the chief, his place was put off-limits, and subsequently he was robbed twice. Maybe if there had been an occasional police presence that might not have happened.

This also held true for about half the bars in town, and a couple of other businesses. The chief was feuding with the owners, and the police officers were told to stay away. What was known as a "walk through" just never took place. I would park and walk in and out of each place just to make a showing. This was a real deterrent for trouble makers. It kept them on something of a good behavior because they never knew when a cop might stop by. No cop meant no walk through which ended any deterrent.

I had spent five years in the Army, and I had a pretty good idea how a commander, boss, or chief should conduct himself. I admit I was also pretty naive. At that point in my life everything was black or white. Certain standards were expected to be maintained, and if you were the law, you sure as hell didn't break the law. And to me this is exactly what the chief was doing. I had been working for the town for five months, and had one month to go on my probation. At six months I would be a full time police officer and protected by civil service regulations. However I was also impulsive.

I called the mayor and asked for an appointment. I didn't tell him why, only that it was important. A few days later I met with the mayor and laid out all the information I had obtained about the chief and how he was running the city and the police department. The mayor sat there and took notes, but asked no questions. When I was finished he informed me that he would look into my allegations and get back to me. I was then sent on my way. Here is a rule to live by: always have an independent witness along.

Two days later I was called into the chief's office and handed a document. I looked at it and found that I was terminated from the police department, effective one minute to midnight on the 180th day of my probationary period. I was fired, but had two weeks left to work. That seemed a bit uncomfortable, but I needed the money.

I contact Kyle and the first thing he asked me was, "What the hell were you thinking? Didn't you know that the chief and the mayor are best friends and have been for years?" No! It seems no one bothered to mention that fact to me. Besides, what difference should that make? The mayor runs the city, and the chief works for him. Kyle says that it was common knowledge in town that the chief, who lived outside the city limits, would bring in all of his friends and neighbors when it was time to vote. They would all cast their votes for the mayor or whatever city councilmen was running for office. It didn't matter that they were voting illegally because the chief's relatives worked in the clerk's office and controlled the voting registrations.

I asked if he could prove it and he replied, "Yes, wait until tomorrow."

The next day Kyle handed me a bunch of photocopies of all registered voters in the city elections. Sure enough there was the chief's name along with others who lived in the county not the city. Contrary to law, they were voting in city elections.

Two days later I was contacted by a couple of city councilmen who were on the shit list of the mayor and chief. They asked that I document everything that was going on and they were going to try and have a hearing. They intended to get the chief fired and dismiss the mayor. The next day the entire high school student body held a demonstration at the school and then marched to city hall. The kids all formed up on the lawn out front and most were carrying signs protesting my dismissal. I guess the teens had never had a police officer who was nice to them before. The demonstration did no good other than make me feel special.

I hung around the town for a few weeks after I was no longer a policeman. I took a couple of odd jobs including a stint as a play by play announcer for a local radio station. I broadcast all the high school football games, and did some advertisement for a few local businesses. The chief started putting pressure on the owners, and before long I couldn't find any work.

The city councilmen, who were against the mayor, planned a meeting and invited me to attend. They informed me that they would back me financially if I hired an attorney and started a recall campaign. I contacted a well-known law office in Tacoma, and the recall papers were filed against the mayor and several city councilmen. Petitions were started, and in a very short period of time, enough signatures were gathered to force a special election. It looked like there would be a vote by the people of the town, and the mayor and his cronies would be gone. I may have taken a brief vacation to Fantasyland.

A few weeks into all of this, I took the written examination for the City of Tacoma Police Department. The test was administered in this huge auditorium at Stadium High School. There were well over three hundred applicants taking the test, and I thought that I didn't stand a chance. I talked to several guys before the test started, and all of them were college graduates. Once the test began, I breezed through it again and was among the first people to finish and leave. This time I felt I had done much better on the exam.

I was talking to friends about my situation and several advised me to contact some organization named the American Civil Liberties Union. I had never heard of them, but my friends assured me that they would be interested in my case and a law suit against the city I had worked in. My pals kept saying things like “discrimination” a word I had never heard uttered.

One fine day I picked up the phone book and looked up the number for the “ACLU.”

“Hello. ACLU.”

“Hi. I got into a beef with the chief of police and the mayor in this small town and they fired me. I have been discriminated against.”

“Oh Wow! Tell me all of the details.”

Which I did.

Then I heard, “Are you a brother?”

“Why yes I am. I have two younger brothers and two younger sisters.”

“No man. Are you a brother?”

“Yes. Are you an idiot? I’m not sure I want your legal help.”

“OK. Let me ask again. Are you a brother?”

“Pay attention. I have two brothers so that makes me their brother. I have two sisters which makes me their brother. My mother and father got married and had five children, one of which is me. So I am a son and a brother to my brothers and sisters.”

"Don't ever call here again."

Click.

I sat around home and waited and a couple of weeks later, I was called by TPD. They informed me that I had finished in the top five on the written test, and they were conducting my background investigation right then. A week went by and I got another call, asking me to report to TPD for a polygraph examination.

When I arrived in the basement of the County-City building I was met by the Staff of the Police Academy. Present were Captain McDonough, Lieutenant Henderson, and a Detective Samuelson who was going to administer the polygraph.

They told me that they had finished the background investigation and had conducted several interviews with my old boss, the chief. They said at first they considered not even talking to me because of what the chief had told them. Then he continued telling them more and more, and by that time they were convinced he was lying. So the logical conclusion was to bring me in and ask me for my side. "We figured no one could be as bad as he made you out to be, and not be in jail."

We all sat around and they fired questions at me regarding my time with the small town police department. The detective took notes and when we finished with the oral interview he stated that he was now going to conduct the polygraph. All the questions on the exam were to confirm I was telling the truth about what had happened with the other police department. There would also be some general questions that all candidates were asked. He took me into a small room and wired me up to the polygraph machine and the test was started.

"Is your real name Clem Kadiddlelhopper?"

"Have you ever been convicted of a felony?"

"Have you ever smoked marijuana?"

Then we moved on to all the questions regarding my previous employment.

"Did you have sex with a farm animal in your police car?"

"No! The sheep is lying."

"Did you continually eat for free from every restaurant in the town?"

"Burp!"

"Were you drinking on duty in the police car, while riding around with a hooker, who was naked except for wearing your gun belt?"

"She wasn't totally naked. I believe she may have had on six inch stilettos."

That was how ridiculous the accusations were. No wonder TPD was convinced the chief was a liar.

I got all finished and the detective informed me that I had failed the polygraph, and would not be hired. I felt like I had been kicked in the groin. I told him that there must be some mistake because I answered every question truthfully. He said that I had passed with flying colors on every question except when he asked me if I had ever smoked marijuana. I said again that I never had, and he replied that every time he asked me that question, the machine said I was not being truthful. After some thought he then asked: "Have you ever thought you have smoked dope?"

I then told him about the time in Vietnam when a Montagnards soldier had given me a hand rolled cigarette, and I later thought it may have been marijuana, but I never knew for sure. We then went back into the polygraph room and he hooked me back up. The only question he asked when we were ready was, "Have you ever knowingly smoked marijuana?"

"No!"

"Okay! You passed."

I then had to take a medical examination and the requisite physical test. I passed everything with flying colors, and a few days later I received a letter welcoming me to the Tacoma Police Department and giving me a start date for the academy. I was also given a courtesy call from the TPD Chief's Office, and was told that by hiring me they expected me to drop all legal action against my former boss and the mayor. I eagerly agreed.

BIG CITY BLUE

It was almost Christmas 1970, and I received the best present I could have gotten; I had just started the police academy. There are about twenty of us in the class and I am the only one with prior experience, if you can call it that. One of my classmates is an old friend, Pat O'Malley. Pat grew up in my wife's neighborhood and she had known him since grade school. I attended high school with Pat and we got reacquainted when we took the police entrance exam together. Pat's father was also on the department and was assigned to the police jail. He had been on the force for years.

On a daily basis we have Sergeants' Monty Laughlin and Phil Sessions as our instructors. Other people will drop by and give us specific classes tailored to their job. We will be given classes by officers and specialist from the laboratory, detectives, traffic, special investigations, dispatchers, and the jail personnel. We will also receive briefings from other law enforcement agencies such as the Military Police, FBI, Sheriff's Office, and the Washington State Patrol.

I had been issued two new uniforms, which included everything except shoes, socks, and underwear. I was also issued a set of navy blue sweats. We ran every day and performed physical training. Pushups, sit-ups, and jumping jacks accompany every two mile run up to Wrights Park and back. I also received a Smith and Wesson .38 caliber revolver, holster, gun belt, handcuffs and case and two ammo pouches. Last, but not least, was the requisite night stick. I spent a lot of hours practicing at home learning how to twirl the stick so I wouldn't smack myself in the head or crotch.

In the basement of the County City building, the police department had its own firing range. This is where everyone would get their initial marksmanship training. Later, I spent a lot of hours at the outdoor police range located on the tidal flats of the city. Not only would I fire my pistol at the standard targets, but I would learn combat shooting. I ran to barricades and learned to fire right and left handed. I was taught to shoot and quickly reload and fire some more. Then I came back at night and did everything again. The class also learned how to load and fire the shotguns that were kept in every police car. Most important, we learned how to put the shotgun in the car and take it back out without shooting a hole in the roof or your partner.

The best part of training was the high speed pursuit classes that were held at an abandoned part of Salishan. Salishan was originally a housing project built in the early 1940's to house war workers and military families. When finished in 1943, it had 2000 housing units. A large section was now nothing but vacant streets. The houses were gone, and the police department was using the area to conduct the pursuit classes. The only thing we ran into here is each other and a curb or two. Some of my fellow trainees just couldn't seem to get the hang of driving fast and sliding around corners. Those of us who grew'up with cars and were street racing as teenagers had no problems. The two or three others keep wrecking the cars and having difficulties.

During the final couple of weeks of recruit training the class was paired up to work with senior patrolmen on a regular shift. These assignments are nerve racking because it is a known fact that the regular officers can get someone dismissed from the academy. If you show cowardice or stupidity, or violate some infraction, you could find yourself unemployed. It was rare, but it did happen. A senior patrolman may drive right back to the station and kick the rookie out of the car. He then would tell the sergeant he would not work with the new guy and doesn't think he will make a very good police officer. That can be all it takes. Or he told everyone else about the rookie and the rookie was then a marked man for the rest of the year he will spend on probation. During that year, he can be dismissed for any reason or for no reason at all.

The class got assigned to work night shifts and everyone was apprehensive. There are senior patrolmen that you just don't want to have to work with. They have a reputation for being really hard on recruits, or generally just being assholes.

The first name on everyone's list was Bud Madera. No one wanted to work with him as a rookie. This cranky old dinosaur walked around with a scowl, and usually had a cigar stuck in the middle of it. He wouldn't even talk to people he liked, and he doesn't like rookies. I looked at the list. Madera/Lazares. Oh shit!

The usual shift briefing was something like this: “Sit down. Shut Up. I’ll do the driving. Don’t touch anything unless I tell you to. Don’t ask any questions. If I want you to know something, I’ll tell you. You do the writing, and don’t make me have to correct it. If we have to fight anyone, you had better back me up.”

For some reason we just clicked. Madera was interested in my Army experiences and of course word had gotten around about my previous police work. He had questions about that. During our shift we handled the usual fights, chases, reports about this and that, and even a couple of hours of boredom. When we finished for the night we turned in our car and shotgun and headed down to the locker room to change. I was sitting on the bench in front of my locker and Madera walked around the corner.

He said, “Do you have change?”

I answered, “Yes.”

He said, “Go upstairs and buy a couple of cokes.”

I didn’t know what to think, but I didn’t want to piss him off now. I ran up to the 2nd floor and got two cokes out of the pop machine and returned to the locker room. Madera took the two bottles into the bathroom and poured 2/3 out of each. He then came back, went to his locker and got out a bottle of rum. He then filled up the bottles and handed me one.

Number One! I'm on probation.

Number Two! I am sitting in the police station, in uniform.

Number Three! There is absolutely no drinking allowed anywhere in the building.

I took a nice big healthy swig and didn't say a word. I was pretty sure that this was a test and I just passed.

After twelve weeks of training I took my final exams. These tests were held over several days and included pistol qualification, high speed driving, and written exams covering felony and misdemeanor law, police policy and regulations, and report writing. A large part of the test also included knowing every street in the city. There were a billion streets and you had to know them all.

"Hey rookie! Give me directions to the corner of Lonely Street."

"Well I think you have to go…."

"Ah! You dumb shit. Tacoma doesn't have a Lonely Street. It was a song by Marty Robins. You rookies couldn't find your ass with both hands."

At the graduation ceremony I learned that I was the honor graduate and finished first in my class. As a reward I was issued a brand new Smith &Wesson .38 cal. Combat Masterpiece. The department just ordered these as replacements for all of the old weapons, and I was issued the very first one. I also got my pick of assignments to one of the patrol squads. I picked the swing shift. That was where the action was.

The guys with seniority and a chance to coast are all on the day shift. The go getters are all working nights. Fresh out of the academy I was just a gypsy. All the squads working nights had two man cars. Some of these partnerships had been going on for years and no one broke them up. Us new guys were used for fill-in if someone was sick or on vacation. Or we were partnered with the squad jerk who couldn't keep a partner. There were guys, who for whatever reason, could not get anyone to work with them. There were drinkers, shirkers, perverts, peepers, and just plain lazy individuals that no one wanted to be with. I got all of them as my partner at one time or another.

"O.K. rookie. Wait in the car while I go check the bicycle seat on that girl's Schwinn for evidence." Sniff! Sniff! Sniff!

I had to spend the next nine months on probation and some guys would test you to see if you're police material. They would throw you into situations to see how well you handled yourself. They might want to get you into a fight to see if you are tough enough. They will put you into a compromising position to make sure they can trust you.

I was working patrol in the south end of the city one night and had one of the old timers as a partner. We got called to a house regarding the theft of something and of course I was doing the writing while he was doing the driving. Normally when you had a report to write, you would do it in the car if you were busy. If you weren't too busy, then you would head for a coffee shop or restaurant. That way you had a nice steady surface to write on and your partner could flirt with the waitress. This night my other half tells me not to write anything just yet. He then drove to an apartment complex. We got out and walked upstairs to an apartment which he then opened with a key he took from his pocket. I had no idea what was going on, but I thought maybe this is where he lived. I walked in and there was a couch, T.V., kitchen table with a couple of chairs, and in the back room was a bed. There was nothing else to show signs of anyone living there. I got pointed to the couch and told to start my report. He went into the kitchen and returned with two beers. I got handed one and not a word was being spoken. Ah ha! This was another test. I drank the beer and wrote the report. Later we were back in the car and he then told me that he and three other cops rented the apartment as a little place to get away, and as a love nest. This had not been covered in any of my classes in recruit training.

I got assigned to the downtown car and was working with a really nice veteran. He treated me like an equal, and was not demeaning or belittling. We were assigned to the swing shift. Things were just starting to get warmed up when we got a call to rush out to Northeast Tacoma for an accident. Normally the patrol cars don't get sent to accidents unless the Traffic Units are tied up. They told us to run Four Bells, which was lights and siren the whole way. I figured it must be bad. We arrived on Marine View Drive and found a one vehicle crash. The car had been coming down from the hills above the bay and hit a telephone pole head on. We rushed to the car and found one occupant. It was a once pretty young woman. Now her face is smashed and bleeding, but the worst part is that she is impaled on the steering wheel shaft. I don't see the actual steering wheel anywhere, but the shaft was shoved into her chest quite a ways. All we could do was hold her head up so she doesn't choke on her own blood, and was hanging onto her hand and telling her she would be okay. We desperately needed an ambulance and the fire department to cut her free. I've called twice to dispatch on the car radio to hurry things along, but we were not hearing any sirens coming.

Then dispatch informed us that the ambulance and fire truck had come out East 11th street, but had gotten stopped by a raised bridge over the Hylebos waterway. They have now turned around and have to take the long way around to get to us. I ran back to inform my partner and I saw him smacking the injured lady in the chest with his fist. He told me that she had quit breathing about three times and the only way to re-start her was to hit her chest above her heart. He and I took turns keeping this lady alive for about fifteen minutes, and then we couldn't get her to respond any more. I smacked her about four times, but nothing. Then the ambulance and fire rig pulled up and they tried to get oxygen into her, but were unable. They got no response from her and then stated, "She's dead."

Then they cut the steering column off and put the body on a gurney with the post sticking up in the air.

We did an accident investigation and found out that the lady was a bartender at the Cliff House Restaurant at the top of Marine View Dr. She had worked all day and then sat and had several drinks when she got off. She got into her car and made the fateful drive down the hill. This would be my first fatal accident scene, but it would not be the last.

It was a night shift around dinner time, and I was working the Hilltop area. This was a square mile of houses and small businesses. It was up the hill from the down town area, and home to most of the minority families. This was also a high crime area for drugs and crooks in general, and at this time the department was also dealing with the Black Panthers. The city had gone through some recent shootings and mini riots, and cops were being targeted. Anyone working up there was nervous and kept their head on a swivel. You needed to see trouble coming before it arrived. One early lesson in the academy was to emphasize the fact that you never stood in front of a door when you knocked. It was a good way to get shot from someone inside.

Our unit got a call to an address on the Hilltop for unknown trouble. It could be a shooting, stabbing, family fight, runaway kid, or not being able to get any channels on the T.V with the rabbit ears.

"O.K. Wrap the tinfoil around the ends of the antenna then lift your right leg 12 inches off the floor. Now turn your head to the north and face Seattle. Don't move. You should be able to see the Mickey Mouse Club with no problem."

We arrived in the area, turned all of our lights off, and coasted to a stop a few houses from the address of the call. When we got to the house we found that it was raised about three feet off the ground on a foundation, and it had this little tiny porch. There was no room to stand to the right side of the porch because of a tree. My partner pointed to the left side and told me to stand there while he got on the porch and knocked. I was standing on the ground in the flower bed with my back to the house. He knocked a couple of times and then I heard the door open. "Oh my god!" I heard from my partner. I don't know what he has seen, but I needed to find out quick. I spun to my left to face the door and the inside of the house, and came face to face with a naked lady.

Well! It wasn't exactly face to face as I was standing about three feet below her head.

"My god! Look it's a wooly mammoth. Can I shoot it?"

The two of us followed her into the living room where she proceeded to sit on the couch and put both feet up on the coffee table. I was trying not to stare, but this was going to be one tough interview. I told her to go put some clothes on and she replied, "Kiss my ass. This is my house, and if I want to be naked, I'll be naked." She finally told us that the reason she called was for us to kick her husband out of the house. He had gotten drunk. She was in the mood and, "The miserable asshole can't get it up."

"Protect and Serve". It says so right on the police car door.

A few nights later on the Hilltop I got a call about a stabbing. We rolled up to an old two story home near the corner of 21st and K Street. It was pitch black out, and I saw someone sitting on the porch. I lit up the area with my flashlight. This large lady was sitting there in a house dress and I walked up and asked her who was hurt. This woman went about 300 pounds buck naked, and buck naked is not what I wanted to see. She stood up, turned around, sort of

bent over, and pulled up her dress.
"See officer. Right here is where that son of a bitch stabbed me."

Smack in the middle of her left butt cheek is a cut about an inch and half long, and it's deep enough that the skin is pulled away. Of course a blind man couldn't have missed this target. We followed her into the house, down the hall and into the kitchen.
She said, "I was just cooking up a mess of greens, and minding my own business when that fucker runs into the kitchen and for no reason, stabs me in the ass."

My partner has been wandering around the house and has found this little old man sitting in the living room watching T.V. This guy didn't go more than 150 pounds, even if he had rocks in his pockets. He looked to be about seventy years old, which is thirty years older than our victim. Our suspect informs us that he is married to the victim, and that he did in fact stab her.
According to him, "That loud ass bitch just wouldn't shut up and let me watch the news. So I jumped up and stabbed her. Here's the knife."

She won’t press charges, and she won’t go to the hospital. I was thinking she needed to have stitches, as there is no way she will be able to slap a band aid on the wound. She hasn’t been able to reach that part of her anatomy since she was twelve.

The sergeant showed up and advised us to just take the male half of the problem somewhere else so he would be out of the house. We loaded him up and the two of them waved bye-bye like they would never see each other again.

DOWN TOWN BEAT

I had often heard that during the 1940's and '50s Tacoma had a reputation for being one of the worst cities in the U.S. It was located close to Fort Lewis and McChord Air Force Base, and not all that far from Bremerton Navy Yard: it attracted a lot of problems. Wherever the military was hanging out there was sure to be bars, gambling, prostitution, and all the crime associated with it. Back in the bad old days, there were bootleggers, whore houses, gambling dens, and just about any other vice you could name. By the time I began working in 1970, the town had calmed down some, but there were still a lot of problems. The downtown area had more than its share.

Tacoma still had some cops walking the beat, and usually at least one crew driving the paddy wagon. Traditionally these jobs were held by the biggest, baddest, meanest sons-of-bitches the department could find. The guys working the down town area took no prisoners in the literal sense. A cop might walk into a dark bar or hallway and find himself immediately in a fight. He had better be able to win or hold his own until help arrived. Those were the days before portable radios. The city had call boxes an officer could use, but you had to be able to get to it, open it with a key, and then hope someone answered on the other end. All of this while trying to hold onto one or more arrestees. Or you might open the call box and find that the phone was gone. This was often done to make room for a couple of bottles of whiskey that the beat guys needed to stay warm during the long cold, rainy season.

The paddy wagon crews all had reputations which they enhanced at every opportunity. One crew made it a special effort to drive around and pick up every street walker they could find on Friday and Saturday nights. They then would jump on the freeway and head to Seattle as fast as they could drive. Once they finished the forty-five minute drive north on I-5, they would dump the hookers and then high tail it back to the city. Of course, Seattle PD was doing the same thing, but it made for a change of scenery and some new faces in town. In its own way, it helped control the prostitution. The girls were off the street for a few hours either going to Seattle or trying to get back.

Another paddy wagon crew were avid hunters and would head off to the port industrial area with a couple of shotguns and a box of double ought rounds. They would finish their shift with a wagon full of geese or ducks, and on one shift they shot a deer. Tough to explain to the sergeant why there are feathers and blood all over the back of the truck.

"Jeez! Sarge. It must have been this way when I checked the wagon out. I would sure ask the day shift crew who the hell they killed".

The paddy wagon was used primarily for transporting the crooks and drunks that the beat cops arrested. On a busy night a crew could have several people in the back waiting their turn to go to the jail and get booked in. It would be so busy that they couldn't break away to make the trip up the hill. The beat guys sometimes got into fights or had a hard time arresting someone. There would be too many witnesses to the arrest, so the cops couldn't get their pay-back on the street. The beat cop would pass the word to the wagon crew and a little justice would be assessed on the way to the station.

The paddy wagon would get up a head of steam going up the hills to the police department. They would bounce over the intersections of Commerce and Market then hit Fawcett and

Tacoma Ave. A loop would be made around the County City building and the wagon would go back down the hills, again bouncing over every intersection. That wagon would be literally air borne at times. The guys in the back would be ricocheting around like ping pong balls. This while also banging into the seats, floor and ceiling and each other. Then the crew would yell loud enough for the crooks to hear, "Watch out for the dog" and slam on the brakes, piling everyone against the wire cage in front. Finally they would arrive at the jail, but sometimes it was a side trip to the hospital for stitches first.

I came into roll call one Friday night and was informed I would be working the wagon downtown. The purpose of these assignments was to find out what kind of fighter you were, and if you would always back up your partner. You didn't work the paddy wagon and not get into fights on Friday and Saturday nights. I was partnered-up with an old timer, and we headed up to the police garage to check out our ride.

Next I had to go through the litany given to each rookie, "Get in. Sit down. Shut up. Don't do anything unless I tell you to. You write and I'll drive."

In reality, I had earned a lot of trust from my different partners. Word had gotten around that I had previous experience as a cop, and the veterans all talked among themselves about which rookie was a keeper and which ones to watch. So I wasn't getting as much crap as some of the other guys from my academy class.

That night we headed down the hills to the Pacific Ave. area. Sometimes we would park and cruise a few of the bars on foot. Being seen is a big deterrent of trouble. The wagon stayed within a two or three block area unless we got a call to respond somewhere else. During that evening and night we handled the usual calls for transporting drunks, a couple involved in a fight, and to pick up a hooker or two that the Vice Squad had pinched.

Dispatch called and informed us that the beat cops had made an arrest at Esmeralda's Bar. This was a rowdy joint near 14th and Pacific Ave. They had a couple of people in custody and needed them transported to the jail. We double parked the wagon and walked into the bar. They had three people under arrest for fighting, one of whom was a 250 pound prostitute. I got handed her and told to load her into the wagon. She wasn't wearing handcuffs, but I figured this was no big deal. Most of the time we didn't cuff anyone who wasn't causing a problem.

So I took her to the back of the paddy wagon and opened the two clamshell doors. I had just gotten her up on the back step when she decided she wasn't going to jail. She spread her legs wide and put a hand on each side of the door way and braced herself. I'm standing at eye level behind her giant ass, while my partner and the beat cops have the two guys they arrested standing on the sidewalk.

This is a typical night with a couple hundred people standing around with nothing to do but watch the cops arrest someone. I had attracted a crowd to my part of the street, and they are all yelling and making crude remarks. The guy I'm working with is telling me to get the woman into the back of the wagon and to quit screwing around. I put a hand on each of her butt cheeks and start to push. She started squirming around and telling me she wasn't going anywhere, which caused me to yell at her and push harder.

Then I slipped. My feet slid back, and my right arm shot between her legs up to my shoulder. I immediately knew this was not going to be my “finest hour.” She was wearing a dress and I’m now under it somewhere. The next thing I knew she clamped her legs together, crossed her ankles, then she squatted down. I’m trying to brace myself and I’m pulling like crazy to get my arm out from between her legs. Now the hooker is moaning and groaning and acting like she is having an orgasm. “Oh! Oh! Oh! I’m cuming. Faster officer; faster”

The crowd is really into it now giving her encouragement, and she is playing to them. I next heard from the cops on the sidewalk: “God damn it Lazares. Put that woman in the wagon.”

My face is plastered to the big ass, but I manage a turn. I looked and they are laughing so hard I thought they would lose their prisoners. My biggest fear was that this is one of those stories that will have a life of its own. I’ll be the brunt of the station house jokes until they find someone else to make fun of.

Then, as abruptly as she decided she wasn’t going to jail, my arrestee stops with all the antics, stands up, and starts into the back of the paddy wagon on her own. She turns to me and says loud enough for the audience to hear, "Thank you officer. That was the best time I have ever had."

The crowd on the street all applauded. We finished loading up, and then it was off to the jail. I also had to make a detour to wash my arm.

I was picked on for two weeks and no one would shake my hand. Then some other rookie did something equally stupid, and it was his turn in the barrel.

GRAVEYARD

I was assigned to work the 11p.m. to 7 a.m. shift and that can be one boring time. Everything that can happen will happen, between the hours of sunset and when the bars close at 2 a.m. So the first few hours of the shift would fly by with call after call. After that you needed to really scramble to find things to do.

If you worked District Four this wasn't a problem because at 3 a.m. Frisbee's Bakery started bringing out the day's donuts. Almost every night of the week there would be anywhere from two cops to eight cops sitting at the big round table in the kitchen. Coffee cups were kept full and donuts hot out of the fryers would be dropped in the middle of the table. There was nothing tastier than mainlining cholesterol straight to the heart. It would be about sixteen more years before the donuts and other vises would bite me in the ass and I would get to take a peek down the "bright tunnel."

We would sit there until someone got a call, or until the sun started coming up. We didn't want all the citizens seeing the patrol cars parked there all night so we would filter out around 5 a.m.

Guys working this shift were also adept at catching a little nap somewhere off the beaten path. There was more than one embarrassed unit who had fallen asleep in some alley, only to wake up and find a paper boy or milkman staring at them through the window.

The most famous incident occurred one night late in the shift. The dispatcher kept calling for the north end car, "John 3-3! John 3-3!" and getting no answer. This went on for five minutes with no one calling dispatch back. Finally John 3-3 came on the air and answered dispatch.

Dispatch came right back with, "John 3-3 we need you to check on a report that a police unit is stuck in the middle of the intersection of 6th Ave. and Union Street. A citizen reports that the patrol car has been just sitting there through about ten light changes!"

"John 3-3 is close by and we'll check."

This was followed by about ten seconds of silence and then,

“John 3-3 checked the intersection and there is no police unit there.”

Late that night we talked to the guys working John 3-3 and they admitted that they had pulled up to the red light on 6th Ave and immediately fallen asleep. They woke up to horns honking at them, and finally heard their call sign on the radio. It took them two seconds to solve that mystery.

Another late shift crew had an even better way to chase the night away. They carried a suitcase in the trunk of their patrol car, and as soon as things slowed down they would pull in somewhere dark and take turns getting re-dressed in civilian clothes. Then the officer dressed in civvies would get dropped off near a bar and go in and buy a case of beer. They also knew where to find a couple of the local groupies. Cop groupies always wanted to go for a ride in a police car. You always knew when that car wasn’t available because no matter how many times they were called, they never answered. These guys had been on the department for years and knew every hideaway in the city limits. They spent their slow nights drinking beer and getting their nightstick polished, but if someone needed help or back up they were always there.

I remember a story about these two. They were sitting in a bar in a Chinese restaurant, and the owner told them they had to leave. It was 2 a.m. and he wanted to close up and go home. They argued for a few minutes with the two cops not wanting to quit drinking and call it a night. The owner stood there pointing at the clock behind the bar, and kept saying, "Two O'clock! Go home!"

With that one cop whipped out his service revolver and shot the clock off the wall.

"See! It ain't two o'clock!"

The owner then said, "Here are the keys. Lock up when you leave."

We also had our share of cops who were peepers and perverts. They spent the entire shift going to every parking spot in the city. They made a science out of being able to coast into the bushes and then sneak up on a car with steamed up windows. They'd then light up the interior of the car with their flashlights hoping to spot someone naked. This became their mission in life. Most of us were bragging on ourselves about how many felons we captured, or the high speed chases we were in. Not these guys. There would have been hardly any crime in the city limits if they had devoted as much time looking for crooks as they did looking for naked teenagers.

Cops became highly creative in inventing games to play on these lonely nights when no calls were coming in. One of the favorites was hide and seek. We would designate a section of the city approximately one square mile, and would then hide in that area. The other crew, usually Gary Wiegand and Ed Loughrey had to find us. There were rules such as: no parking inside somewhere like a garage. You couldn't cut down a tree and camouflage your car, nor could you go buy a can of paint and redo the paint scheme.

One night my partner, a guy named Yerbury and I were the crew that would hide. I got stuck with him for a couple of weeks, but it seemed that he was like minded. If there was fun to be had, count him in.

We finally found this really out-of-the way alley and decided we would back down it. We could see that it dead ended up against a building. Yerbury was carefully backing up when all of sudden the windshield of the cruiser was pointing straight up in the air. The city was putting a sewer line in and had dug a nice deep hole across the alley. The back of the police car was down in this hole a good five feet and it was not coming out.

We had to walk to the nearest phone booth and call a tow truck. We met the driver out on the main street and after threatening him with being shot, he backed down the alley far enough to hook us up and pull us out. He was sworn to secrecy and given a lifetime free pass to commit small indiscretions. Wiegand and Loughrey had by then been attracted to all of the lights and found us. They too were sworn to secrecy and we promised to handle their shitty calls for a week.

About two weeks later, we decided to pay those two back for all the crap they were giving us about our little incident. I was assigned to District Five and they were assigned to the adjacent District Four. My partner, Yerbury called them on the radio and asked where they were. They answered that they were sitting in a coffee shop at 45th and Pacific Ave. We then told them to meet us at the Tacoma Mall, assuming

they would travel on city streets and then come across I-5 using the 48th Street overpass to arrive at the mall. We set up our ambush. We filled two balloons full of water and parked on a side street next to the pedestrian overpass on 48th. We crouched down behind the railing and waited Pretty soon here came our pals. As they got near I jumped up and dropped my balloon hitting the front grill of their patrol car. Yerbury was just a tad slower getting his balloon up and over the guard rail. As I watched, his balloon hit the windshield and exploded.
"That is my version, and I am sticking to it."

We ran for our car and got there just in time to hear them screaming on the radio that they may have been shot or bombed. They said their windshield had been blown out and they needed back-up right away. Of course, we responded that we would be there as quick as possible. I mean we were parked a half-block from where they were sitting. Every police car in the city showed up to look for the "ambushers" and the sergeant was taking statements from the two soaked victims.

As soon as things calmed down, the victims of the bombing came over and informed us that they had seen us as soon as we stood up on the overpass. They now owned us forever. They drove to the station to replace their vehicle which had no windshield and was a tad drafty while I tried to find out what the statute of limitations was on this prank.
Gary Wiegand kept this story a secret from 1972 until 2013. He hadn't even told his wife. A true brother in blue.

Another night and another partner. We got a call about 2 a.m. on a suspicious car parked in the hills overlooking I-5. The area had not been developed yet and was several square miles of hills, trails, trees, and Scotch bloom. Everyone with a car used it for parking and necking, but sometimes other things were going on. Stolen cars would get stripped out there, and a safe from a burglary or stolen property would show up from time to time.

That night we killed our lights and started slowly into the area. Up ahead we could see the car pulled into the bushes. All the windows were fogged-up and we could see one person on the driver's side sitting up. There was a lot of activity inside the car and it was kind of bouncing up and down a little. We eased in behind it thinking it was kids making out and we would just hit the spotlight to announce that they weren't alone. I really didn't need to see naked teenagers, and I usually gave them a chance to get their clothing re-arranged before making contact with them. But you always needed to see who was in the car. There may be a pedophile or a rapist involved in some hanky panky. With a little luck it might even be a fellow cop administering a "field breathalyzer test."

The guy I'm riding with shined the spotlight on the back of the car.

"What in the hell is that?" we both shouted.

Lying on the ground behind the driver's door are about five chickens, and they are not moving. We got out and approached the car, one on each side with our flashlights checking the back and front seat. What we saw inside the car was an older male with no clothes on and he had a chicken "impaled" on his wee wee. In the back seat are half a dozen live chickens patiently waiting their turn to go up and down on this guy's shift stick. Talk about freaky! This perv was screwing chickens to death.

“Hey sergeant! We need to see you out here in the woods, and bring the rule book with you. I think we may have a ‘Hen-ocide’ here!”

The next thing everyone heard on the police radio was, “Buck buck buck buuuuuck! It’s Chicken mannnn! He’s everywhere! He’s everywhere!”

DAYLIGHT

The only daylight I've seen in the last month has been when the cloudy, crappy, rainy, drizzly, fog started getting a little less gray around 6 a.m. Then it was check-in the patrol car and shotgun and go home and try to sleep. I had a room all set up in the basement and it was darker than the inside of a whale's ass. I would go to work in the dark. Come home in the dark. Sleep until supper time which was also dark, and then play with the kids until it was time to go to work at 11 p.m. Or at least I tried to sleep. All the normal daytime things continue around you and it is difficult to really get any sleep. The phone was ringing or someone was at the door. One of the kids has a boo-boo and is crying. Family or friends have dropped over. It's a normal day for everyone else, while it was my sleep time. Upstairs was the little clomp-clomp-clomp of Heleen and my two girls Michelle and Monica. We had a new baby at home, Michael, but he wasn't up and clomping yet.

Michael arrived about a month ago while I was on a day shift. I no sooner got into my patrol car at 6 a.m. when dispatch said I was needed at home, “Get there now! Your wife’s water has broken!”

I ran with lights and siren to my house which was about twenty minutes from the police station. This day it was about five minutes from door-to-door. I loaded Heleen into the car and again used lights and siren to take her to the hospital. We arrived at Tacoma General and because of the police car screeching to a halt in the driveway, I had all the assistance I needed to get Heleen inside.

About a half hour later, my sergeant arrived and told me that he had my District covered and I could stay at the hospital until the baby was born. A short time later a nurse informed me I had a perfect baby boy. Heleen was all pissed-off because she wanted to be the one to tell me, but the nurses wouldn’t think twice about telling some cop he was a new daddy.

I got rotated around to the day shift. I would now have a more normal life, except that there was nothing to do during the day time. You spend all day going from place-to-place writing reports. Every crime that happened at night that wasn't reported at the time has now been found. Burglary reports from businesses that were broken into, garbage cans that were stolen from the alleys, the car that is supposed to be parked "right there," but is now missing, the fifteen-year-old girl dating the twenty year old soldier, and was not in her bed this morning. Usually a day shift was eight hours of writing one report after another. It would be so busy sometimes that you had to take shorthand notes to tickle your memory later. You could finally take a break and, over coffee, write three or four reports from memory. Occasionally though, day shift could become very interesting.

"Code 30! Code 30!" Officer needs assistance immediately. Everyone would drop whatever they were doing and respond lights and siren. It was supposed to be just the closest officers and no lights and siren, but when you are bored you go.

"Code 30. I am at 72nd and Sheridan and I have a lion here. I have shot it several times, but it is still coming at me."

What the hell? We all raced over to find that this veteran officer was minding his own business when a lion appeared in a very menacing manner. The lion refused to surrender and get into the back seat of the police car, so the officer shot all of his bullets at it. He then panicked and grabbed his shotgun with the four rounds of double ought buck, and pumped all of them down range at the beast. He then locked himself in his car and called for help.

It was about this time when a man walked up and began calling, "Fluffy. Fluffy. Here boy."

Fluffy was a forty pound yellow poodle which had been given a really cute haircut to resemble a lion. Thank God the cop couldn't shoot straight with the runny stuff in his pants. Twelve rounds of .38 and four from the shotgun. If and when he ever lived this down, he'd be at the police range practicing.

One boring day shift I was working a patrol car in District Four when I spotted a motorcycle going about 100 mph in a 30 mph zone. Hot damn!

"Tacoma. This is 4-4, and I'm in pursuit of a motorcycle going south on Alaska Street."

I had my lights and siren on chasing this guy everywhere. I kept calling the direction and streets, but no one was close enough to help me corral him. Every time I would get close enough, the bike would shoot through a field or across a lawn or two and elude me. This chase had been going on for about ten minutes which is a pretty long time. I was now going south on Alaska Street again and the bike was to my left going across all of the yards on that street. I had finally had enough and drove up on a home's front lawn and smacked the bike in the rear tire.

The bike spun around about three times and launched the rider up and over my hood. I slammed to a stop, and jumped out to handcuff this guy if he was still alive. A traffic unit which handled all accidents had arrived, and I was now maybe in trouble for denting the police car and killing the motorcyclist. I started to explain, when this little old lady pulled up in her car and got out. She walked over and told the traffic investigator, "I saw the whole thing. This officer was just trying to get the motorcycle to pull over when all of a sudden the motorcycle ran right into the police car. He did it on purpose too."

"Why thank you ma'am. Let me give you a big, wet kiss because I know I love you."
The shit-head on the motorcycle was sixteen and still breathing, so he got a ride to the hospital and then booked into juvenile detention.

I seemed to have had a real penchant for rounding up crooks using my cop car. One day I got a call that there was unknown trouble at the University of Puget Sound Field House. When I arrived, I found out there had been an assault by a young male on another person, and that an officer was in foot pursuit of the suspect. I spotted them running through the huge parking lot and the officer was losing ground. You can be in great shape, but try running in a uniform with a gun belt, while wearing dress shoes. Meanwhile the suspect is picking them up and laying them down in his felony Keds. I picked an intercept angle and hit the gas.

The kid running was too busy looking behind him and waiting for the police officer to collapse to see me at all. When he woke up he said the last thing he remembers was he had observed the City of Tacoma Seal, and the words Police Department on a car door somewhere. The winded cop was only more than happy to tell the sergeant that the suspect deliberately ran into my parked police car.

One of the most prevalent calls on day shift in the early 70's was missing children. They were not so much missing as more like a runaway, and it was primarily the female of the species. The boys usually took off from a screwed-up home life and no one bothered to report it. Girls were different. Mom couldn't wait to call the cops and make a report about their little sweetheart being missing. By the time you spent a half-hour getting all the details, it was easy to figure out that the darling was shacked up with a guy somewhere. A lot of them were also heading to San Francisco or some other big city to join the flower children.

We had this infamous patrolman named Squeaky who was usually working in the jail. He was invaluable there because he had a photographic memory for faces, and he could recite a crooks entire pedigree to include all his family, friends and last known addresses. You would haul "Mr. Shithead" into the booking area, and start to process him when Squeaky would walk over and say, "Hello! If it isn't 'Donald Dickweed.' I haven't seen you in about three years. I arrested your cousin 'Little Larry the Loser,' and he's doing time in Walla Walla. What name did you give the nice officers this time?" Things were not CSI fast in those days. You would book a person and then get him fingerprinted and photographed, and it might take a few days to find out, that the guy has already bailed out, and was on the 10 most wanted list. This happened very frequently.

Squeaky was filling-in on day shift and it was always an experience to watch him work. He had like a 100 years on the job and was tolerated for all his foibles. One of which was that he never had an unlit cigarette. Any time you saw Squeaky, he had a butt in his mouth with about two inches of ash hanging off the end. Another of his character traits was to always say exactly what came to mind. If he had a thought, it was immediately becoming words spilling from his lips. The cigarettes, though, would almost kill Squeaky.

I got a call to see a woman about a missing teenager. Squeaky got on his radio and stated he was going to be assisting me on the call. He must have been bored. We arrived about the same time and went up together, and knocked on the door. A lady answered the door and led us into her nicely furnished living room. Squeaky was walking around the carpet with his usual cigarette dangling from the side of his face. It has almost burned to the end, but the ashes were still there, looking like a two-inch long, gray caterpillar. The lady noticed this and grabbed an ashtray and started pursuing Squeaky around the room. She finally got him cornered and reaches up to place the ashtray squarely under Squeaky's chin. Squeaky removes the cigarette from his mouth and calmly flicked the ashes on the carpet. I moved into a better position in case I had to catch the lady when she fainted, but this was just the start.

After the lady picked up the offending ashes she explained that her little fifteen year-old daughter is missing and has been gone since the day before. Squeaky asks if she has a boyfriend, and mom said, "Yes."
Then I heard Squeaky say, "You know these girls all do their thinking with their pussy. As soon as it starts to get itchy they take off with some guy. If she doesn't come home in a few days call us again," and he walked out the door.

I was now looking at a hyperventilating mother who I know is going to call the mayor and chief of police, so I do the only thing I can think of. I covered up my name tag with my hat and followed Squeaky out the door.

A couple of days later, I was almost off shift, when I got a dispatch to see a man about a theft report. When I pulled up, there was Squeaky again looking to help out. We went up and knocked on the door and a voice yelled, “Come on in.”

We walked in and found this guy standing in the living room in only his underpants with an oxygen tube hooked to his nose. There was a large tank of air and about 100 feet of tube running around the room. Squeaky walked up to the guy and stood about a foot away, and began asking questions. Of course, Squeaky had a cigarette hanging out of his mouth and I was sort of worried he was going to blow us all up. I was standing to the side and watching all of this.

Within a minute or two, our complainant started revolving and fell to the floor in a heap. I looked at Squeaky and asked what the hell happened. He says he doesn’t know, and then I look down. Squeaky was standing with both feet on the guy’s oxygen line.

There was a policy in place at this time with the City of Tacoma. If you worked for the city, you had to reside inside the city limits. Squeaky got thrown out of the house by Mrs. Squeaky, and had no place to live. He got a small ten foot camp trailer and parked it behind a restaurant on Puyallup Ave. He plugged into their electrical power and had the trailer situated next to the phone booth out back. Another policy was that you had to have a telephone so the department could always call you. Squeaky gave the number of the pay phone to the desk sergeant.

Squeaky came home one night, but had failed to shut off the propane when he left. The camper trailer had a few hours to fill up with gas and was just waiting for a chain smoker to show up. They say that when the fire department showed up, they found a ten foot long section of floor, two wheels, and a singed Squeaky standing there in his underwear. Everything else was gone.

One day at turn out, I was informed that I will be working at the station that day to learn how the calls are answered and then dispatched. There was a small room with phones and two or three cops stationed there to answer them. Messages were written down and then stuck on a small conveyer belt going to the next room to the dispatchers. Or you could push a buzzer and the dispatchers would pick up the phone and hear the conversation first hand. This was necessary if it was an emergency, like an armed robbery or a shooting.

Sometimes a female would call and start talking dirty. That was also classified as an emergency so everyone got to listen in on that conversation.

"Hi Officer. I want to come down there and pull out your big police whistle and give it a toot."

"Yes Ma'am! Get a paper and pencil and I'll give you directions."

Then you would give her your name, which almost always was the same as the chief's.

"Isn't Lyle Smith the chief's name?"

"Yes it is. But I spell mine differently. Lil Smyth."

I was in the little message room when the phone rang and I picked it up to hear a woman telling me, "You need to get these men out of my house. I'm tired of them coming over here and constantly having sex with me."

I have now pushed the buzzer. I ask her how many guys we are talking about and she says a couple of dozen. I asked her to explain how these men all know about her and how to find her.

She replied, “They got my name and phone number from either in men’s rooms or phone booths.”

I then stupidly asked, “Well! Who is putting your name and number in all of those places?”

She said, “I am.”

This conversation went back and forth for a while and then I got this bright idea! Officer “He Pissed Me off Last Week” is working today and he’s in that district. “Let’s send him to her,” and we did. We later heard from him that this crazy lady is living with about fifty cats and there is cat food and kitty shit from one end of the house to the other. Plus, as soon as he walked in the door, she tried to corner him and chased him all over the place trying to get his gun belt off. This address and story made the rounds really quick and from that day forward every new rookie got sent to the “Cat Lady’s” house for a little training session.

I showed up the next day to work the phones again, but the sergeant called me into his office and gave me a new assignment. There had been an armed robbery at a pawn shop out on Portland Ave. The husband and wife who ran the place had been shot. He survived, but she died. Before they went down the husband pulled his gun and shot the robber.

Now both were in surgery at Tacoma General Hospital and they wanted me to go there. I was handed a portable tape recorder and told to get a dying declaration from the robber. I drove to the hospital and found the surgery area, and told them why I was there. The nurse in charge looked at me like I had just sprouted a second head. She asked if I was sure I knew what I was doing. I told her that my boss told me to come and record the robber, and that is what I was going to do.

They made me dress in hospital scrubs to include a hat and booties, and then had me wash up. I was then led into the operating room where they were working on the robbery suspect. I walked to the head of the table so I can get his death bed confession and looked down. This guy is on his back and has been split from his wiener to his windpipe. He is wide open and looking a lot like a canoe. Everything has been pulled out and parts are laying everywhere. I was thinking, "This guy is not telling me or anyone else anything for a while".

Then the doors flew open and a nurse came in and told the doctor, "The man this guy shot is taking a turn for the worse." The surgeon looked down and said, "Fuck him," and with that the whole surgical team left the operating room to go work on the pawn shop owner. I stood there for a minute or two and then shut off the recorder and walked out of the operating room. I got out of my hospital clothes and went back down to the station, where I informed the sergeant that the guy just didn't want to talk.

Day shift was okay but I missed the action going on at night. Plus, I seemed to get more than my share of calls of "Baby not breathing." This was before they had identified the Sudden Infant Death Syndrome. People would wake up and find their new child just laying there in the crib. The call would go out to the police department, and I would race over there as fast I could. It could be black, white, brown or yellow families. It didn't matter. Every ethnic group was hit. I would rush into the house to find a frantic mother or father holding a limp child. I would grab the baby and start doing

CPR, but knowing from the chilliness of the body that I would not be bringing the baby back to life. Imagine the stress on the police officer racing across city streets as fast as his car could go, then rushing into the home knowing that the chances of finding the baby alive were slim and none. Doing CPR to no avail, and then having to tell the family that their baby is gone. Ever wonder why cops drink?

This was the early 70's and so of course, I let my hair grow out a little long, and re-grew the mustache I had through my years of flying. I had shaved it off when I joined the police department, and I missed it. I also became involved in cars and motorcycles again. I began dragging home different cars to work on, then figured I needed a motorcycle.

Not just any motorcycle but a chopper. "Easy Rider" came out in 1969, and I just knew I had to build something that looked cool. So I picked up a Honda and moved it into my basement. It took a little maneuvering and a lot of disassembly of door frames, but I finally got it in there. Then I tore it apart. By just keeping the engine, I started to fabricate my dream bike. This bike would end up having a hard tail and extended front forks. I added a small seat and ape hanger handlebars. I was the proud owner of the most uncomfortable bike I have ever ridden. But I was looking good.

I also traded a really nice 1967 El Camino for a 1958 Corvette. The Corvette was delivered to the house on a trailer. It was a complete car, except it had to be assembled. The body was sitting on the frame and everything else was in boxes. I got the car on a Friday afternoon and had to have it running by Monday so I could drive it to work. I bolted the engine to the frame and set the body back on top. I threw a seat inside and did enough wiring to make it start. As I sit here today it's been forty-two years since those days, and on occasion I still hear from Heleen, "What piece of crap have you drug home now?"

I can't seem to stop buying fixer uppers.

Though I was fulltime T.P.D, I was still in the Army Reserves and flying helicopters from Sand Point Naval Air Station, which was located on Lake Washington in Seattle. This is how I financed the motorcycle and auto parts I needed to buy. Flying in the reserves was great. No one was shooting at me, and my flying time was usually spent on cross country flights. I would crank up a helicopter and get someone to fly along. Then we would head down to Ocean Shores, land on the golf course, and stroll across the street for a beer and a sandwich.

I did have an incident one time that got me a medal from the military and an award from the police department. I had to do an annual check-ride with an instructor pilot to show my competency and skills. I went out to Fort Lewis and met the instructor and we checked out a Huey and departed for the evaluation ride. I did some pattern work at the airfield and then did a few touch and goes into small landing zones out in the fields and forests of the Army post.

I was flying near Highway 507, a two lane road, from the Spanaway area to the small town of Roy. I looked down at some smoke and saw two cars that had just hit head on. One was on its side and the other had flipped to its back. The nearest help was miles away. I got on the radio to the McChord Air Force Base tower and told them to call for help, and that I would land and assess the situation.

A couple of cars had stopped by then as I landed in the grass next to the accident. I left the helicopter running and ran to the wreck. I found that a car with six drunken Indians in it had crossed the center line and hit a car with two people. There were a couple of Indians pinned under a car and we had no way of getting them out. They also appeared dead to me, as did a couple of people who had been thrown from the cars. I did find two who looked critical, and I thought they might not live if they didn't get help quickly.

I guess it was all a Vietnam flash back. I ordered the crew chief from my helicopter to fold the rear seats, as I told him we would transport the injured. I then got all the people standing around to help me carry and load the two critical into the back of the Huey. A nurse who was driving by, left her car and climbed aboard, and with the crew chief they began administering first aid. The Huey carried a large first aid kit on the rear wall. I lifted off and turned toward Tacoma.

I called McChord again and asked first for permission to overfly their field for a direct route into Tacoma. I then instructed them to call the St. Joseph Hospital and tell them I was inbound with two critical auto accident patients.

St. Joes had just recently installed a heliport in a field across the street from the emergency room. I was to be their very first real live medivac. When I made my landing, doctors, nurses and orderlies were there to unload my two patients and rush them inside. I then flew the nurse back to her car on Highway 507, where there was now a large gathering of State Patrol Officers doing a fatal accident investigation. I reported to them what I had done with the other victims, and then lifted off to resume my check-ride. The instructor said: "I have never done anything like that in my life. I just fly around the U.S doing routine crap. I believe you have passed your check-ride. Let's park and go to the club for a drink. I'm buying"

He later reported the flight through the Army chain-of-command, and I got a pretty ribbon for saving the lives of the two victims. The state patrol called the chief's office and I ended up with another "Atta Boy" from TPD.

Written reprimands were ‘pinkies’ or an ‘Ah Shit’. It took three ‘Atta Boys’ to wipe out an ‘Ah Shit.’ I never came close to breaking even.

ME AND BOBBY

I had been doing a pretty good job and it became a regular occurrence to have different sergeants requesting me to work with their squads. There was one shift I really wanted. It was 4th Relief. The hours are from 8 p.m. to 4 a.m. and everything happens then. If you work 4th, you got all the "hot calls," robberies, assaults, shootings, stabbings, theft or burglaries in progress. The time just flew by. Plus, with all the arrests, you are called into court a lot. With the abundance of crime comes a lot of overtime at night, and then there are the hearings and trials. The courts all happened during the daytime, so more overtime.

Finally Sergeant Dick Raymond asked me if I wanted to come to his squad and work 4th Relief. I jumped at the request. Maybe I should have given it more thought. This squad would end up with one officer in the funny farm and three more officers doing time for child molestation. A fourth officer would kill a guy in a card game and do life without parole. 4th Relief was staffed with about sixteen patrolmen and about four of these would end up taking their own lives in later years. Sounds just like the guys I shared a tent with in Vietnam. There were about ten of us flying together in 1967. Three are left alive. The rest all managed to destroy themselves one way or another.

I showed up for my first "turn out" in the basement of TPD. We had a large room with a pool table, a couch or two and some chairs. I stood around getting my bearing and looking at the new group of guys I would be working with.

In one corner were four officers, and one of them is shouting at the others.

"I'm telling you, we were cornered in that bar by at least four Zoosters."

His partner responded, "I think it was more like six Zoosters."

I have been a cop for over a year by this time including the small town stint, and I have never heard of a Zooster.

I moved closer.

"The god damn Zoosters were everywhere. Then when things started getting real interesting, a Spinner came walking in. How was I supposed to deal with Zoosters and Spinners all at the same time?"

I was getting dizzy, but before I could bang my head against the wall, the sergeant called everyone to order and gave out the assignments.

That night, as soon as I got with my partner for the shift, I had to ask him to explain what I thought I heard in the turn out room.

He said: "Everyone who is on the streets and is an asshole is a "Zooster" to that team. One team calls everyone "dick heads" and another team calls them "scrotes" and, of course there is the ever popular "dirt bags."

"Okay. I understand that, but now what is a Spinner?" I asked.

"A Spinner is a crazy person. Everyone knows that."

"Whack jobs, nut case, ding dong, whack-o, tutti fruity, and space case. I'll just add Spinner."

This was just one of the interesting nights in the turn out room. We had a patrolman who had served in Vietnam in the Marine Corps, and he was what one would call "wrapped a little tight." Now that I had new words in my vocabulary, I would call him a "Spinner."

We were all standing around and a couple of guys were playing a game of pool. Officer "I should be on Thorazine" was staring into space and having some flashbacks to his time in the jungle.
"I had Zoosters and Spinners and gooks in the wire. They were everywhere and they were aiming to kill us all. It was dark and I could hear them screaming at me that they were coming. I started shooting as many of them as I could but there were just too many."

Then some dumb shit cop thought it would be funny as hell to shut the lights off and scream, "Gooks!" There was an instantaneous blackout and banging and shouting. The lights got turned back on and there stood "Officer under Medicated" on top of the pool table with his gun out. I was not waiting to find out just who he intended to shoot, so I began digging a hole in the linoleum. His partner finally got him calmed down and back to reality so they could go out to the streets and chase real Spinners and Zoosters. If they wanted to meet later at an Asian restaurant, I thought I would pass.

This officer would in later years be medically retired for

being crazy. It was rumored that he sandbagged his house and cut fields of fire in all the vegetation. No one was sneaking up on him. He eventually loaded all of his guns in a bag and drove to Sea-Tac Airport with the intention of flying to Washington D.C to discuss problems with the President. He may still be doing small spins in a room at Western State Hospital.

I became part of the team and moved from guy to guy. Everyone had their regular partner, but people are off sick, or on vacation, so I filled in. I moved around from car-to-car until one day I was paired up with Bob Yerbury. We had worked together a few times in the past and had got along just fine. This is like a match made in police heaven. I started a sentence and he finished it. He began a thought and I knew what it was before it became words. I would call him and tell him what I was going to wear to work so he could copy me. More importantly, we knew a crook when we saw one. During the next few years, the two of us had one of the highest arrest records month-after-month for felonies and other crimes. We knew just where to look for stuff happening, and if it had already gone down, we knew where to find the crooks that did it. A lot of it was luck, but by using good instincts you put yourself on the right spot for luck to find you.

Bobby and I were also innovative. The two of us may have been the first bicycle patrolmen anywhere. I had never heard of bike cops, but one night I decided to bring an old bicycle to work. I stashed it, and after we began our shift, I loaded it in the trunk of the police car. My thinking was the police car was just too visible and noisy, plus you couldn't sneak up on anyone. We hauled the bike out to the south end and would take turns riding up and down alleys with it. There were a limited number of walkie talkies available to each shift, but one of us would always grab one so we could communicate with each other. We started capturing prowlers and thieves in the act and generally scaring the crap out of a lot of potential crooks.

Sometimes the two of us would also go into a business district and get access to the roofs. From there we could then watch what was going on below us a couple of blocks away and burglars loved to enter through the roofs. We made plenty of really good arrests by watching someone stealing a car, or breaking into a business. They could never figure out how we caught them. It was fun watching from on high as some bandit would look left, then right. Then turn around and look in every other direction, but never look up. It just never occurred to them.

Another great patrol trick Bob and I used was to look for suspicious cars. We just had this knack for picking the right car. It was probably what we referred to as "Blue Fever." Our police cars were painted blue and when a crook saw the car, they would break out in a sweat. If they were up to no good and you came by them, or pulled up near them at a traffic light, they just couldn't resist trying not to look at you. There they sat in their car staring holes in the windshield. They wouldn't even look at each other. They were so intent on being invisible it made them stand out all the more. Everyone looks at a police car. Not these idiots.

"Please don't see me. Pretty please. Oh god! The cop just looked over here. He knows I've got drugs in the car. I'll just bend over and stuff the shit under the seat. Damn!"

Cue the lights and siren.

"O.K. asshole. Grab a piece of the curb. Do you just want to hand me the weed or would you rather I tore the car apart looking for it?"

When we spotted some car obeying the law "letter perfect" we would keep following them forever. No reason other than they were driving too well. They just couldn't stand the tension any longer. The window would come down and a bag of weed would fly through the air, and then they would hit the gas. The chase was on and we always won. I don't remember anyone ever getting away from us. The radio is faster than a car, and a city full of cops itching to do high speed runs really put the odds in our favor.

Sometimes we would make them run from us, just so everyone on duty could be involved in a high speed chase. The trick to this was to find a car with people in it that you could tell were up to no good. Something they did or didn't do made them a target. I would follow them long enough for them to know they had my attention. Then I would start falling back. Slowly I would drop a half block, then a whole block behind them. Then I flipped on the lights and siren. There could be one hundred reasons I have just activated my emergency equipment, but not to them. I could only be after them, and they were not going to stop and wait to find out what I wanted. The chase would be on. All the patrol cars would join in, and we would be sliding around corners, and racing up and down streets. It was a real adrenalin high, and very addictive and just great "cop fun."

Bobby and I had a reputation as being fair with all the people we came into contact with. The two of us didn't like being what was referred to as "badge heavy." Some cops arrested people just because they could. We let a lot of little fish go with our brand of street justice and so earned a lot of respect, plus a lot of people who would assist us later with information.

A lot of the city hadn't been developed yet so there were large tracts of nothing but bushes. The young people would pull in there and drink beer, and then dump all the empties and trash in the bushes. We devised a way of helping Mother Nature while helping ourselves to new sources of information. We would pull in quietly and get behind a car full of kids, then hit the lights and illuminate them. We would get everyone out of the car and ID them and check ages. Now was the decision time for them. They could choose to go jail or to go home. They were always given the choice. When they picked the "let me go home option," we informed them that as a public service they should pick up their trash, and they were more than happy to comply. Bob and I would assemble them and have them round up every can and bottle that was theirs. They would scatter and then come back each carrying several beer bottles and cans. This is when they would be told that they had the wrong ones. We would get the look from them while they dumped all this trash in their trunk. They would then scamper off to find more, and this would be repeated until;

1. They had run off the effects of the beer and could now drive.
2. They had done their civic duty and cleaned up the trash in one square acre.

We would then follow them to a dumpster where everything would be thrown away. I think they all realized that we could have taken them to jail, and they got the easy way out. These kids never failed to talk to us, and of course they were never back parked in our district drinking beer.

This same treatment was afforded to those caught with a baggie of marijuana. In those days, it was a felony to have any on you including seeds and stems. I just could not take someone to jail for a little grass providing it was recreational and they did nothing to talk themselves into getting arrested. More people let their mouth get them arrested, when if they had showed a little common sense, they could have gone home that night.

"I believe your alligator mouth just overrode your hummingbird ass. Step back and place your hands on the car. Feet back and spread 'em."

I would stop some guy for speeding or DWI (Driving While an Idiot) and, when the window came down, you knew they had been toking. Then you convinced them it was easier to hand us the MJ than having their car impounded and searched. If they just had a small amount we would offer the option of:

1. Go to jail.
2. Beautify the streets of Tacoma and obtain a healthier lifestyle.

Invariably they would select number 2. The handcuffs would come off and they would be pointed down the street where they would be shown a traffic light approximately one mile away. They would be told that they were to run to that traffic light and along the way sprinkle the marijuana. We would meet them at the light to inspect the baggie and then we would hand them back their car keys. By the time they were done, I don't think too much of the high was left. Plus, they saved themselves a felony arrest and a car impound. We kept their names in our little book and they now owed us information.

Not all drugs were "just a little grass," and not everyone got off with exercise. There was a lot of acid being dropped and it did really strange things to people. When we found acid, they went to jail, and the same for those using PCP.

One call that always got our attention was, "Any unit in the area. Report of a naked lady running in the street." Every patrol car responded and you tried to be the first to arrive. The reason for this was that I never saw a pretty lady running naked. It was always some skank that was better off with her clothes on. If you got there first you would grab the naked lady and then wait for some unsuspecting fellow officers to roll up. The lady would get stuffed into the back seat of their car, so they could deal with her. Nothing was sweeter than to meet the two cops later for coffee and listen to them tell you about how the naked stoned female scrunched up on the seat and pee'd on them over the security screen. Of course, they now owed Bobby and me and we went around a lot watching our back and waiting for payback.

"4-1 is in pursuit. We are chasing a '57 Ford westbound on 38th street."

"4-2 is going."

"4-4 is on the way."

Bob and I started moving in that general direction. We are waiting to see which way the Ford is going next so we can intercept.

"We are now going south on M street," yelled 4-1 on the radio.

We cut across 46th street and as we get to M, we saw them go flying by. 4-1 is right behind the Ford and 4-4 is behind 4-1. We fell in the back and as we got to 54th , the Ford turned right and then took a left down the alley. I told Bob to stay on M and we would cut the Ford off when it came down the alley. This was a perfect plan from my point of view. The Ford driver had a plan of his own.

Bob blocked the alley at 56th street and I started to get out the passenger side. My intention was to point my gun at the driver to make him stop. I looked up and he's coming at me doing about 50 mph, and he didn't look like he was going to be putting on the brakes. All I could see was this giant behind the steering wheel. I mean, this guy was so big he blocked vision out the rear window. I gazed soulfully into his big brown eyes and realized this guy is going to kill me. I jumped back into the front seat and closed the door just as he plowed into us. Not having time to buckle in, I bounced like a ping pong ball all around the car. The entire side of the car was smashed in as was the front fender. We are out of the chase. The Ford slid to the right, and then headed off down 56th street with everyone else still chasing him. They finally got him stopped two blocks later and he was hauled off to jail. I would meet this guy one year later with a whole different ending to the encounter.

It was a late shift in the south end. Bobby and I were cruising northbound on Pacific Ave and it was getting close to quitting time. It was around 3 a.m. and the streets were deserted. As we approach 72nd street, a car flew past us at an estimated speed of 80 mph. I'm driving and immediately gave chase while Bob got on the radio and requested backup. I had the lights and siren on but the driver would not pull over. Finally, around 62nd, I pulled up on his left front and started squeezing him to the curb. I looked over and there is one guy driving and one guy in the back seat. What the hell is this I wondered?

The driver slowed to about 15 mph and rolled down his window. He yelled at us that he had a gunshot victim in the back seat and was heading for the hospital. Bob told him to get behind us and we would lead the way. The nearest hospital, Puget Sound, was about two miles ahead and that is where we are going. We pulled around to the back of the hospital where the entrance to the emergency room was located. The car that was following us pulled in next to us and another police car with two officers parked behind the parade.

The guys in the car got out and we rushed over and pulled open the rear doors. Lying on the seat is a naked female with a neat round hole in her right boob. I grabbed her hands and Bob and another officer each grabbed a leg. They began pulling her out by her legs, and still hanging on to her arms,

I started through the back seat. As her butt cleared the doorway, Bob and the other cop were pulling in two different directions, and her legs were spreading wide. I was half way through the back seat and I looked up at them and blurted out, “Make a wish.” They started laughing and almost dropped the poor woman. Meanwhile we were getting death stares from the two guys who were with her. I guess not everyone appreciated cop humor.
We got her inside the emergency room and the staff took over. A few minutes later a nurse came out to inform us that the lady was dead.

We took the two men aside to find out what was going on. Cop humor was put on hold because now we had a death investigation to conduct. We discovered that the younger of the two was the husband, and the other was the husband’s father. The story came out that they had been drinking all night at a neighbor’s trailer. At some point the father went back to his trailer and after a while the husband followed, leaving his wife at the neighbors. The husband went to sleep and a short time later the father got his pistol out, and then walked to the neighbors to see what his daughter-in-law was doing. When he got there, he banged on the door and it was opened by daughter-in-law who was now buck naked. The father-in-law took one look and shot her in the chest. He didn't even wait to find out what the daughter in law had been doing. She was guilty beyond reasonable doubt. Realizing what he had done, he woke up his son and they loaded her into the car for the drive to the hospital. We arrested the father-in-law and called out for detectives to handle the follow up.

The 4th Relief was never dull. I worked five nights a week and every night was another story. We had our share of fires and One that was different and stayed with me, happened downtown. Being out at night cruising around you would smell smoke and track it down to a house on fire. Or you might see the glow of a fire reflected in the front windows of a building. The Tacoma Fire Department put out their calls of a fire somewhere, and we might be a block away and so be the first to arrive. A couple of these fires have stuck with me all these years.

The call came out over the police radio of an apartment fire downtown. We were really close and drove over to assist. Normally a police car was used for traffic control, but if a crime was suspected, we would become involved. As we pulled up, we heard a frantic yell that there were kids in the apartment. It was an old, two story wood structure, and the fire was contained in the lower living room/kitchen area. I had three kids of my own, so there were no second thoughts. I ran into the apartment and raced up the stairs to the bedrooms on the second floor. The first open door on the right showed a baby's crib, and I headed for it. As I looked inside the crib, I spotted what looked like a charred baby's body. A dead kid was always the worst, and one that was burned up was especially bad. I lost it right there. I started to gag and was ready to throw up. A second later a fireman pushed me aside and reached into the crib. He came up with a lifelike brown rubber doll, and threw it at me. If I could have seen well enough to shoot him, I would have. Instead, I went down and hid in my patrol car before anyone found out my name.

Another night in the south end, Bobby and I were just driving up and down side streets looking for bad guys. It was probably 2 or 3 a.m. and nothing was moving. Then we smelled smoke. We were in the area of 72nd and East J Street, and started looking everywhere. We saw smoke coming out of a single-story ranch style house, parked, and ran to the front door after telling the dispatcher to call the fire department. I started banging on the front door, and Bob was rattling the windows. Pretty soon the front door opened and a lady staggered out wearing pajamas. We put her into our police car. That's when she started screaming: "My baby! My baby!"

Bobby and I rushed into the house. I couldn't see a thing. The whole interior was filled with smoke down to about a foot off the floor. We dropped down and started to crawl toward the back bedrooms when a fireman appeared behind us. He kicked us in the ass and told us to get the hell out of the house. On the front porch, we met more firemen and told them the lady was screaming for her baby. Bob and I then ran around to the rear of the house while the firemen went in.

A few seconds later there was a crash from the bedroom we were standing near and a large metal cage came flying through the window. It landed at our feet and the biggest, most pissed off Iguana I have ever seen came racing out of the cage. I figured I would let Bob and the fireman capture

“Baby” while I retreated to the police car.

We started going to so many fires that I began taking cooking lessons, and lifting weights. I also started my own construction company, and learned to play racquet ball.

UNDERCOVER-- SORT OF

I usually drove my chopper to work, and I was usually wearing my uniform. This tended to really piss off the sergeant, lieutenant, captain and chief. Did I miss anyone?

As I pulled into the station one day I was met by the narcotics sergeant, who had no idea what my name was, but he had a question for me, "Hey! With that motorcycle, do you think you could buy drugs?"

I said, "Hell yes!"

I was not about to tell him that I had no clue as to how this was done

Wow! A chance for me to get out of uniform and work undercover. This was my lucky day. I got dismissed from patrol duty and then I got briefed by the narc's. They told me that they have had a problem with a bike gang showing up in the Point Defiance Park and doing drugs. They have tried, but have been unable to get close to the group. The gang seems to end up in the park most afternoons and hang-out in the beach area of Puget Sound. I got sent home with some money in my pocket and told to change clothes and then go to the park and buy drugs. Okay! I have never bought drugs in my whole life. I had no idea what the hell I was supposed to do. The instructions I got were just a little vague. I guessed I would just wing it.

I headed to the park and pulled down to Owens Beach, parked my motorcycle and then sat on a picnic bench. About an hour later, I heard motorcycles coming. A group of about twenty bikers showed up. They parked, and a few of them wandered over to where I was sitting. Several more were checking out my bike. They looked me over and one of the group sat down next to me.

He then said, “Hey! Man. Do you have any papers?”

Only later would I know that he was looking for rolling papers for his marijuana.

I looked him right in the eye and responded, “No. The Tacoma News Tribune doesn’t come out until later today.”

Did I ever get a strange look? With that they all walked to their bikes and left. I didn’t have a clue what I may have done, but I knew I was not telling anyone. The next day I was back fighting crime with Bobby.

My hair continued to grow and was now hanging down over my collar. I was twenty-five years old and looked about fifteen. No wonder my name was baby face when I was in grade school. A couple of weeks went by and I was approached by the Narc sergeant again. He wanted to know if I wanted to try buying drugs again. I said sure, and could I bring Bob with me? He told me that they have been having a lot of calls about kids buying and selling drugs at Stadium High School, and he sure doesn't have anyone in his squad who could go there and make a buy.

I got handed more money, and Bob and I got excused from patrol to become "undercover drug buyers." Bobby had also been building a chopper, but it was not ready. I couldn't put his big ass on my handlebars, so we needed a new plan. The P.D. didn't have any undercover cars so we had to improvise. I called my father-in-law, Tony, and asked him if I could come by the Barber School he ran and borrow his car. Tony had this '57 VW which ran nice, but looked bad. It didn't even have a back seat. We went by and picked it up, but I didn't tell him why I needed to borrow it. He would have had visions of gangsters coming after him, so no sense worrying him.

Bobby and I drove down to Stadium High and parked in an alley across from the school's main entrance. It took about ten seconds before some kid came by and wanted to know if we wanted to score some dope. Yup! He left and returned about five minutes later with another kid. They both climbed into the VW and sat on the floor in the back, and just that quick sold us a baggie of marijuana. They got ready to leave and I then remember my instructions.

"I will need your names," I told them.

"What?" came the reply.

I said, "How am I supposed to come back and find you so I can buy more?"

So they nodded to each other and spelled their first and last names, what grade they were in, and their mother's maiden name, just in case I had a problem finding them.

We've been gone about two hours from the PD. Upon arriving back, we dropped the drugs on the sergeant's desk. He can't believe it and thinks we must have used our own stash. We finally convinced him and thus began a three week assignment where Bob and I spent every day finding more and more kids at Stadium to buy dope from.

When we finished with this undercover job, it was back to patrol work while the narcotic team rounded up all the kids. Of course, we hadn't cut our hair or shaved in three weeks and had to get cleaned up to meet the uniform standards. No sooner had we reported back to 4th Relief, when we got a message that the narc's wanted us again.

Bobby's motorcycle was finished now, so we decide to start doing the biker thing with the two of us riding everywhere. We were still doing the high schools and had branched out to hit all of them. All we had to do was pull up on those bikes and someone would sell us drugs. It was way too easy. The downside of the bikes was that we could not ride anywhere on the city streets without getting pulled over by a cop. We looked like dirt bags, so we were treated accordingly. Every Sheriff, State Patrol, or city cop that saw us, profiled us, and then pulled us to the curb. Talk about a bad image. I remember pulling up next to a family sedan at a traffic light. The guy driving looked over at the two of us and said something to the family. Mom and all the kids immediately locked the car doors.

All good things must come to an end. Riding around with no one to answer to and sort of working whenever we felt like it had spoiled us big time. No one had been actively working U C and buying drugs. These are always the best cases when they go to court. You have first-hand testimony from a cop that he bought dope from the defendant, and your partner is there to back up all the statements. I found that when some idiot got arrested and charged with selling dope to a cop, they would just plead guilty. It was a huge shock to their system to find out that they even had sold to a cop.

After all, they did ask me if I was a cop before they would do the deal. The word on the streets was that if you asked a cop if he was a cop, he had to tell you or the deal was null and void. Ha. Ha. Ha. Wrong information.
"Are you a cop?"
"Nope."
"Prove it."
"O.K." Zipppp…. "Look at that. Does it look like a two inch, single-shot, detective special to you?"

The courts had already upheld the element that a cop could lie to a defendant in order to gain their trust. They would plea bargain the charges down to avoid the trial, and having to worry about a bigger sentence. Plus, they didn't want to look stupid to their friends.

"You sold dope to who?"

SINGING IN THE TPD CHOIR

Bob and I were back on 4th Relief after our hiatus and we picked up right where we left off. Arrests, chases, fights and fun are the order of the day. Cops build a lot of stress working. It is really tough to just end your shift at 4:00 a.m and go home and try to sleep. So we started having "choir practice" after every shift. Normally someone would bring a bottle of booze to work, but we also relied on "found beer." Each and every one of us knew where the kids were hanging out and drinking. It was easy pickings to hit these spots and confiscate the beer from the teenagers.

Lord knows I lost enough of that to the cops when I was growing up. We used to go to dances out in Lakewood or Steilacoom and just about every other weekend we would get stopped by Sheriff's Deputies. I never got arrested, but they always took some or all of my beer.

"Okay kid. I'll let you go with a warning this time, but I'm going to have to take this beer in for evidence."

"Sure Officer. Put it in the evidence cage right next to the two six packs you confiscated last week."

This kept up for weeks and weeks. Finally one night my pals and I got stopped on the way to St. Mary's parish hall in Lake City for a Friday night dance. The two deputies took our beer and gave us a warning, and then they pulled away. We got turned around in the neighborhood and didn't know where we were or where we were going. The next turn took us down by American Lake, and who should we find, but the two lawmen drinking our beer. I walked over and knocked on the window of the police car. Without saying a word the deputy in the passenger seat handed me two six packs. After that night, we never had a problem with our beer getting confiscated out in Lakewood.

As soon as our shift was over, we would pile into someone's car and park in the TPD lot and drink. If we had Scotch or bourbon, then we would park at the station gas pumps. The water hose would be run from the stanchion through a window and used for a mixer. I remember one night when a team mate brought five pounds of cooked smelt and a bottle of Scotch. The six of us ate smelt and threw the bones and heads out the window. Pretty soon the ground and gas pumps were covered in this crap. I often wondered what the maintenance people thought when they showed up for work that next morning.

"Maybe the fish were spawning and swam up through the drain pipe."

Most nights we would have a couple of beers and call it quits. Some nights though we would still be at it when the sun came up. Then we'd all head downtown to find a tavern opening at 6 a.m. Half the guys would be in uniform so they would just take off their shirts. The gun belts stayed on. Those in civilian clothes were usually wearing shoulder holsters and these would stay on even when their coats came off. So there would be six or eight cops half in the bag, all packing. One would be playing the piano. Two or four would be playing pool against regular customers who were coming in. And a couple more cops would be rolling around on the floor trying to pin each other to the dirty floor. Or the slugging would start. Each guy taking turns trying to knock the other cop off his bar stool.

"Okay. I'm too drunk to walk, so I guess I'll drive home."

"Quit standing on my hand and I'll go with you."

I lived not far from the police station and I had a bar and a pool table in the basement. The guys on the squad started coming to my house. Being tricky, I would go into the house and then down to the basement. I would open the window and they would all crawl in. They were very courteous and quiet because I had a wife and three children sleeping above us. For about fifteen minutes! Then a wrestling match would break out with all the shouting and cursing. The basement door at the top of the stairs would fly open and Heleen would start shouting down that she was going to kill someone if they didn't get their asses out of the house. Guys would scramble for the windows and head for home.

Later we refined our choir practice to also include small arms training, and combat pistol techniques. There were usually about four of us off-shift at the same time. A really good friend named Dave Norton bounced at some of the night clubs and he began singing in the choir. He was ready about the same time we were, plus he owned a convertible. The convertible made it easy to dispense of empty cans and bottles, and when the mood struck, which was often, you could shoot your service revolver straight up to hit street lights. Most of the time we were riding around in uniform anyway, so reloads were handy. I wonder what Sgt. Raymond thought when we came to work about every third night and needed eighteen more .38 cal rounds.

I don't know how many nights calls came into the station about a car load of idiots shooting street lights out on Pacific Ave. or South Tacoma Way. The district car would track us down and beg us to go to another district and practice, or better yet, go out in the county and let the Sheriff deal with us.

One night, we all got called to a very large party that was out of control at the University of Puget Sound. There were underage kids there and lots of beer. We ended up seizing a full keg of beer and taking it to the police station along with the guy who had thrown the party. He was arrested for "Contributing to the Delinquency of a Minor."

The guy got booked into jail and the keg was entered as evidence and placed in the evidence cage. I finished my shift and changed clothes. As I walked up the hill toward my car, Bobby and some others yelled for me to join them for a beer. They were sitting in someone's car up at the gas pumps, so off I went to join in. Just then Sgt. Raymond pulled up in his police car and told us not to leave, he'd be right back. With that he burned rubber out of the police parking lot and headed up the hill. A few minutes later, he came squealing back into the parking lot and pulled in by the station's back door. He went in carrying something and a few minutes later came back out carrying more items. He got back into his car and pulled up next to where we were sitting. He got out of his car and was hauling two, five-gallon, plastic pickle jugs full of beer. He came over and told us to make room, he's joining us.

I turned to him and said, "Sergeant. We don't have any cups for the beer."
He said to hold the beer he'd be right back. He jumped into his car and roared out of the parking lot again, heading up the hill. A few minutes later he slid back into the lot next to us. He got out and had a stack of beer glasses in his hands. We found out later that he had entered the evidence cage and that is where the beer came from. He didn't have anything to put the beer in so he went to a restaurant named Brown's and beat on the door until the janitor opened up. He then grabbed the pickle jugs and emptied them into the sink, washed them out, and then came back to the station for the beer. He made a return voyage to Brown's when we needed glasses. He should have gotten an award for being enterprising. He also should have gotten us snacks.

A month later we got called into court for the trial of the guy who had thrown the party. Judge Roland was presiding. He ran municipal court since sometime in the 1800's. One of the officers went down to the evidence room and carried the keg into the court room with one hand. The defendant looked at the keg and turned to the judge and said, "Your Honor, that keg was full when they took it from me." Judge Roland didn't miss a beat and replied, "Evaporation."

Bobby and I could do no wrong as far as Sgt. Raymond was concerned. If we wanted to do something special to fight crime, or we wanted to move our hours around to work a special criminal element, Raymond would allow it. We did test his patience and resolve a few times though.

One night Bob and I were working the Four District as usual, but somehow found ourselves about eleven miles north of that area. It was a very nice spring evening, and we decided to cruise Five Mile Drive in Point Defiance Park. Besides we could get back to our district by using the lights and siren if need be. We were slowly driving through the woods when all of sudden Bobby slammed on the brakes, threw the door open, and jumped out. I then watched as he went running into the bushes and trees. A few seconds went by and I heard him yelling, "Open the trunk!" I pushed the trunk release inside the glove compartment, and a moment later I hear the trunk slam shut. Bob got back into the driver's seat, and I had to ask, "What in the hell was that all about?"

I got a one word response, "Raccoon."

I then asked him what he was talking about and he replied that he had captured a baby raccoon and was going to take it home and make it a pet.

"I want one, too."

"What?"

"You heard me. If you have a pet raccoon, I want a pet raccoon."

The car door flew open and Bobby disappeared into the brush again. A minute went by and I heard, "Open the trunk!"

Pop! Slam! We now had two baby raccoons in the trunk of the police car.

We were still at "Pet Central" when we heard over the police radio: "4-4. What is your location?"

We mumbled in reply hoping they didn't get more specific. We were then directed to proceed downtown to 15th and J Street on a report of a dead body. We were driving toward the address in no big hurry, and our two furry pals were running all over the trunk of the car. We pulled up to stop lights, and people were staring at us because of all the strange sounds coming out of the back of our car. The raccoons were making these animal noises and banging around. I was sure the citizens who saw and heard this thought we had some crook tied-up and locked in the trunk.

We finally arrived at the dead body call and parked out front. We went into the apartment and met the fire department paramedics who said it was an elderly man, and he probably died of natural causes. We walked back outside to our car and there are about fifty people standing around looking at our car. This area was located in the Hilltop, and at the time was where most of the minority citizens lived. They are all standing there talking to each other and listening to the police car making all these funny sounds. They, like everyone else, figured we had someone locked in the trunk, but they didn't want to know who or why.

I got on the radio and requested Sgt. Raymond. He answered and wanted to know what I needed. I asked him if he could meet us somewhere out in the field. He said he was at the station and was not going to leave. If we needed to talk to him, we could come down there. Bob drove us to the back door of the police department, and I again got on the radio and asked for Raymond. He answered again, said he was in the sergeant's office and for us to come in there. I told him it would be better if he came outside. A moment later he appeared, opened the rear door of our car and got in. He no sooner sat down when the two bandits in the trunk let loose again.

Raymond looked at us and said, "I don't want to know. Whatever is in that trunk had better disappear. I will take you out of service for one hour. Now make it happen."

Bobby drove us out to his house and we backed the police car into his garage. As soon as we opened the trunk, both raccoons jumped out and ran up into the rafters. We had to get back to our assigned area and figured we would deal with them later. The next day we built cages and caught the raccoons by using fishing net. I took mine home and we each began training them to be pets. Mine got to the point where he was hand-fed by my children. This lasted for about two months. Then one very early morning I heard my door bell ring. I went to the front door and opened it to find a cage and raccoon sitting on my porch. There was a note from Bobby that he was going to Reno for a few days and I could now have his raccoon.

I tried keeping the two of them together but as soon as they got into the same cage they reverted to wild animals. Up to this point the kids were playing with our raccoon and hand feeding it. Not any longer. I was worried they would bite one of the kids, so I called Bob who was now home from his vacation. That night we checked-out a police car and immediately drove to my house. We loaded the cage with both raccoons in it and drove back out to Point Defiance where we let them go with a stern warning to stay out of the city.

There was a surplus store on South Tacoma Way. It covered about a half city block and was crammed full of stuff. It was also easy to break into, and it had an alarm that would go off with a little gust of wind. Someone was always getting sent there to check for a "Burglary in Progress." Most of the time it was a false alarm, or someone had hit the place and quickly left. Everyone was tired of going there and having to search the entire building. It could take a couple of hours. Bobby and I got called to go there about four times in one short span of time. We normally didn't work that district, but if the district car was busy, someone had to respond.

Another night and another call for us to go to the surplus store because the alarm company is calling in. We arrived at the same time as the owner, who unlocked the front door for us. We walked in with our flashlights on, but we thought there was no reason to pull our guns. I took about five steps into the building, and just for giggles I yelled, "All right asshole. Come out with your hands up or I'll shoot."

I was just so tired of searching this business.

Right in front of me was the counter, and from behind it up popped this damn burglar with his hands in the air.

"Don't shoot me! Don't shoot me!"

"I should shoot you just for making me crap my pants."

We had a lot of silly little rules on the department. Some of them were really dumb, but if you didn't follow them you could end up in trouble with the sergeant and lieutenant.

And if you pissed those two off enough, you might end up standing in front of the captain. That was guaranteed to get you days off without pay. At the least, rule breaking would generate a 'pinkie'. This was a written reprimand. There were about three or four copies of the reprimand and the copy you got to keep was pink. The other copies went into your police file and to personnel. One way to generate a pinkie was to be caught without your hat on. While seated in the car or inside having a meal you could take it off. Otherwise it had better be on your head.

There was a large bar fight in a restaurant named "Ben Dews," located in the north end out on 6th Ave. This was normally a quiet family restaurant, but on this particular Friday night it turned into a Donnybrook. A bunch of guys were fighting with each other until the police showed up and then they joined sides against the cops. Anyone not tied-up on a major crime call raced out there to help the cops who had gotten the call. When I arrived, I noticed about ten to fifteen civilians and cops mixing it up, and I started to wade in. It was then I saw one of the cops get his hat knocked off with a punch. He bent over to put it back on, so he wouldn't get in trouble, and POW! He got hit again. The hat flew off and he was on his hands and knees searching for it. He was getting kicked and punched, but there was no way he was getting up without his hat on his head. The poor cop took a beating rather than a pinkie.

The TPD also had issued an order that you were always to have your tie on unless it was summer and you were wearing the short sleeve uniform. Like everyone else, I hated the hat and the tie, and of course I was always getting in trouble with the sergeant for not wearing them. Like all the other cops, as soon as we were done with inspection, and we left the station in our cars, off came the tie and the hat got stuffed behind the seat. But you had to remember to put them back on when you were somewhere the sergeant might drop by. I took to wearing my coat at the inspections and I would keep it zipped all the way up to my chin. I wasn't even making a pretense of wearing the tie. Sergeant Raymond got wise and told me that I had better not be caught at the next turnout without a tie on.

When I had been asked to work undercover, I didn't have any appropriate attire, so I went to the evidence room and rummaged through the large pile of clothes that lay there unclaimed. I found a necktie in that pile that was bright yellow and had a hand-painted picture of a naked redhead on it. I just had to have it and kept it in a place of honor at home in my closet. The next night I took the tie with me to work and when no one was watching I tied it around my neck, put on my jacket and zipped it shut. Raymond called everyone to attention and started the inspection. When he got to me he said, “Lazares. Unzip that jacket and you had better be wearing a tie.”

I undid the coat, and I thought sarge was going to choke to death, but he never bothered me again about a necktie.

Bobby and I were stuck downtown for a shift because the regular car was off this night and no one else wanted the detail. When things are hopping downtown it makes for a short shift. The night just flies by. But when they turn off the lights and roll up the sidewalk, the time can drag. We were driving in circles trying to find someone or something to catch our eye. Then as we drove up Stadium Way, we spotted a car parked in the back of a lot and the windows were all steamed up. We pulled into the lot and shined the lights on the car, and then waited a minute or two. I got out and approached the driver’s side and Bob was covering the passenger door. What we found was two middle aged males trying to get their clothes back on. Neither Bobby nor I gave a crap one way or the other about consenting adults, but we know we had better ID these two and file a F.I.R.

The Field Interview Report was a 3x5 card with all the pertinent information on who you had contacted, where the contact was made, and the circumstances for the contact. Normally these F.I.R. cards never saw the light of day again. We moved these two guys apart and gathered the information, and we then released them. We had found out that both of them were school teachers and worked in the Tacoma School District.

An hour later, the far north end car got dispatched to Point Defiance on a suspicious car. When they arrived they found one dead school teacher with a garden hose running from the tail pipe to the inside of the car. I'm guessing he had gotten a little concerned we were going to tell his employer or family, so he smoked the exhaust.

NO LIFE LIKE THE NIGHT LIFE

I really can't remember a boring night on 4th Relief. Something was always going on. Calls were continually coming in for crimes-in-progress, or to backup another unit. The worst case was when you had to go out and dig up a criminal intent on causing trouble. Bob and I knew every place they were hanging out, or where they lived and what cars they drove. If it was quiet for a while, we would cruise all the known areas until we found someone doing something they were not supposed to.

One night we were combing the alleys and back roads around Salishan when we spotted a Cadillac driven by one of our known dope dealers, Arthur Dean. I was driving the squad car and fell-in behind him.

If you follow them long enough they always do something stupid to get them pulled over. They will throw drugs or guns out the window or commit a traffic violation. Best case is that they decide to run for it and hope you don't catch them.

I finally hit the roof lights and siren and pulled the caddy over near McIlvaigh Jr. High School at 56th and Portland Ave. We were on a little side road that ran past the school grounds. I pulled Arthur out of the car and spread him across the hood while Bobby covered him. During the pat down I found some balloons of suspected heroin and gave them to Bob. I then cuffed our doper with his hands behind him and placed him in the back of our car. Bobby got into the front passenger side and started to log in our evidence and begin the arrest report. I went back to the Caddy to look for more drugs. A few moments later I heard a scream and looked up in time to see Bobby's feet going over the front seat into the back.

I immediately thought that our suspect had gotten his hands back around to the front and had put them around Bob's neck and was choking him with the handcuffs. I bailed out of the car and ran up to the back of our car and opened the door. I was still thinking Bob was being choked to death so I pulled my gun. I was then trying to get the gun up against Arthur's head so I could shoot him. It was dark inside the car except for the dome light, and I couldn't see well enough to get off a shot. I was also yelling for Bobby to hang on.

Then I heard Bob say, “He’s got the dope. He swallowed it.” I yanked both of them out the rear door and then started choking Arthur Dean while also applying some Smith and Wesson to his noggin. Bob got untangled and was helping me strangle and punch Arthur. Bob and I then drug him to the side of the road where there was a huge water puddle. It was a foot deep and ten feet long. Mr. Asshole got pulled right into the middle and I shoved his head all the way under the water. Bob was on top of him and the two of us were doing our damndest to drown Arthur. We pulled him up and he started puking little balloons of dope, so he got punched and dunked some more until we figured we had all of our evidence back.

After we settled down and got Arthur restrained in the backseat, Bob told me what had happened. Bob had the balloons sitting on the seat next to him and he was busy writing the reports. Arthur Dean told Bob that he should warn me that there was a loaded gun under the seat of the Cadillac and it might go off. Bob started to get out of the car to yell at me when the crook slipped his hands from his back to his front and then dove over the seat. He grabbed all of the evidence and shoved it into his mouth, hoping to swallow it. Bob then jumped back into the car and over the seat trying to stop the guy. I came within a hair of shooting Arthur Dean who I thought was killing my partner, and as it was, we beat the living crap out of him. Bob kept a mug shot of him to show other crooks what we did when they failed to cooperate. By the time Arthur Dean was booked his face was swollen, his eyes were black and blue, and his hair was standing straight up in the air. He truly looked like the loser in a face plant contest.

The first time I worked U C, I had ridden my motorcycle down to Owens Beach to try and buy drugs. This group of bikers was the local chapter of the Banditos. They were involved in all kinds of illegal crap and we were always looking for ways to screw with them. One night Bobby and I were following them as they were riding west on 72nd Street. We noticed there were about eight bikes and several had women riding on the back. We also noted that they were having a little difficulty staying upright. We guessed they had ingested beer, drugs, or both and were not doing real well in the balance/steering department. As we started slowing for the lights at 72nd and I-5, we could see them all eyeballing us in their rear view mirrors. We sat behind them at the red light and as the light changed green I hit the siren! Three or four motorcycles guys and a couple of women passengers went ass over handle bars and were sprawled all over the pavement. I pulled the car alongside of them and Bobby rolled down his window.

"You all have a nice night now. We are here to protect and serve."

And with that we drove off leaving them all piled in the middle of the road.

Bobby and I liked to put the screw to the dope dealers up on the Hilltop. The local hangout for the bad guys was this black-owned bar called the Office Tavern. Not too many whites ever went in there unless they were crooks and looking to score. Bob and I would sneak up on the "Office" , turn on all of our lights and the siren, and come roaring up to the front door. We would watch the patrons scattering like cockroaches, almost all of them running for the bathroom to flush their stash down the toilet. This was appropriately called "Cop Fun." We would do this for several nights until everyone was used to us pulling this trick. Then on the next night we would roar up to the front door, stop and get out. We would then start for the front door before thcy all bolted for the toilet. We would calmly walk in, sit down at the bar and order two Cokes, “Leave the caps on please.”

The dope dealers loved to double park and just leave their keys in the ignition. These assholes were all packing guns and knew no one in the neighborhood would think twice of messing with their cars. This did not even slow down Bobby and I in our never ending crusade to screw with this bunch. We would pull up to their cars and yank the keys out. Then the keys got tossed on to the roof of the nearest building.

We also had a technique to be used on the pimpmobiles. These were gaudy, decked-out Cadillac’s and other big cars used by the pimps, hustlers and dope dealers. There was chrome everywhere, plus fur, and in some cases I believe dingle balls. The way to deal with the pimps was to screw with their cars. So slingshots were procured and a stash of ball bearings. If a pimpmobile was found unattended, then it was a simple matter of slowly cruising by and letting fly a steely right through their window.
Crime didn’t pay, one way or another.

It didn't take too many visits to the "Office" before we got called into the station and were told to quit fucking with the business people at 25th and K St. Bobby and I reminded the brass that we were entitled to a break per the bylaws of the union, and we can take that break anywhere we want in our district. It took the brass about ten seconds to consider that and re-assign us back to District Four.

One early evening, I was driving back to the station for some reason which escapes me. I pulled up to a stop at the traffic light at 11th and Tacoma Ave, and in the lane to my right was a Cadillac full of males. Bobby looked over and said, "As I was heading in to work I heard a call about a Cadillac that got stolen earlier today. Fall back and I'll check the plate."

The light changed and as the Caddy went by, there were about seven sets of eyeballs looking at us. Bobby called dispatch and ran the plate. By then we had reached 9th and turned left up the hill with us now behind the Cadillac. Dispatch said, "The car is reported stolen." I hit the lights and siren and Bob yelled; "We are in pursuit of a stolen Cadillac, eastbound down 9th Street." We had been going west, but the minute I lit up the Caddy, it spun a U-turn and the chase was on. I hit the intersection of Tacoma Ave. again and was airborne. The Caddy in front of me is spewing sparks every time we hit an intersection as we raced down the hills. I was airborne again across Fawcett and not coming down until we were almost at Market. The caddy turned a hard left on Market, and I hit the car in the left rear quarter panel. It spun into the curb and parked itself between two cars.

The driver stayed on the gas and rammed his way back onto Market going north. As Market turned into St. Helens the Cadillac ran a police car off the road by driving straight at it. With me and Bobby hot on their tail, they ran the light at St. Helens and Division, lost control, knocked over a light pole, and hit a telephone pole. The pole snapped in two as the Cadillac went airborne off a hill and hit a building between the basement and the first floor. I knew for sure we were going to have to pull about six or seven dead people from the wreckage. By now a lot of police units that had responded, arrived. Everyone went running down the hill into the bushes and trees looking for the bad guys who I figured were squished. Pretty soon they were escorting the crooks up the hill in handcuffs. There were some cuts and bruises, but no one was dead.

I was standing on the street corner taking this all in when a motorcycle cop pulled up next to me and started laughing his head off. I knew a flying car was funny, but not that funny. He said to me, “I took the report on this Cadillac this morning. The guy I dealt with was in charge of VIP’s visiting Weyerhaeuser Lumber. This jerk told me I had better find this car quick, and when it came back it better not have a scratch on it. I can’t wait to call him and tell him he can pick up the Caddy at Bills Towing, Turner Towing, Burn’s Towing, Camel Towing, and whoever else may be needed for all the parts lying down there.”

Bobby and I got dispatched to of all places, the duplex I lived in when I first got married in 1965. It hadn’t changed a bit. It was half way up Fairbanks Hill, and was real exciting to get to when it was icy. We had a report of a lady in distress, but beyond that, had no clue what we would find. When we arrived, we were met by the husband who stated his wife was having a baby, and it was on its way as we spoke.

Never having had this kind of call before, we did what any other dumb shit would do. We loaded her in the back seat with me, and Bob got in front to drive, with the husband riding shotgun. We raced across 38th Street heading for St. Joseph Hospital with the lights and siren going. I was squished up against the rear door sideways and I had the ladies legs, one on either side of me. The lady's dress is up over her belly, and I was looking down at the top of a little head making its first appearance. "Bob I think you need to drive faster!"

I'm wondering if I should maybe get ready to catch the kid, or should I just push it back in for now. The husband is hanging over the seat, not sure what his priority should be. Hold his wife's hand while she gets ready to deliver, or cover my eyes so I quit staring at his wife's crotch. Bob finally slid into the emergency room entrance at St. Joe's, and I was relieved of having to play catcher.

That was exciting, so we needed to unwind and some personal mayhem directed at fellow officers was always the answer. We drove around the Four District looking for a victim when we spotted a familiar pickup truck parked

behind the Mountain Tavern at 56th and Pacific. Hmm! Looks like Sergeant Richburg didn't quite make it home from work. We parked in the alley and then peeked into the bar. There he was, sitting at the bar drinking a beer and regaling people with his war stories.
I thought, "We have time to come up with something."

These were the days of metal trash cans. They were about fifty gallons capacity and had a metal cover with a handle on top. We walked up and down nearby alleys and gathered five or six garbage can lids. We then scrounged around and found a length of rope.

I tied all of the lids to the rope, and then I got under Richburg's back bumper and tied the rope to it. I then stuffed all the lids under the rear of the truck where they wouldn't be seen. Bobby and I took ourselves out-of-service for a meal break, and hid across the street and waited. Pretty soon Jim came out and climbed into the cab of the truck. He only lived a few blocks away, so we followed him. He started out nice and slow, but then began picking up speed. Pretty soon he was sliding around corners with the trash can lids chasing him, until he slid to a stop in front of his house.

He jumped out and ran into his residence. We found out later through the grapevine that when the banging started he thought he was being shot at, and by golly when he looked in the rear view mirror, he could see the sparks on the street behind him. The next day he also discovered the garbage can lids tied to his truck.

"Pinky swear, Bob. We ain't telling him what we did."

Bobby's father was a long time officer on the TPD and was now retiring. A huge party was planned for March of '74, and it was going to be held in the basement of the Holy Rosary Catholic School. Everyone who knew Bob Sr. was attending, including the chief. I wouldn't miss it for anything, even though I had invitation to a bachelor party. I ended up at the retirement party, and was doing my best to drink huge amounts of liquor while filling everyone's glasses.

After having several tall Scotch and sodas, I was approached by Pat O'Malley who said, "You know we are missing the bachelor party and I hear that they have strippers." I loved Bob Sr. and of course I was supposed to be helping my partner tend bar, but there may be other officers in need of backup. Away we went.

Pat and I arrived at the Rodeway Inn out on 70th and I-5, and made our way to the room. When we got about 500 feet away, we could hear the noise down the hallway. When we pushed our way in, it was so jammed with cops we couldn't move. There were stag movies being shown on the wall and I believe a stripper was doing her thing, but Pat and I got shoved into a corner and could not see a thing. I knew there was a poker game going on, but I could never get close. I could only see the tops of the heads in the movie, and there were fifty people between me and the stripper. This is dumb. We stayed about a half-hour and decided to leave. By then the retirement party was over, so I just headed home.

The next day I showed up for work and was immediately called in for interviews by the brass. It seems that there was this large, tall motorcycle cop at the party, and his function was to write down the names of everyone who showed up. This cop was a raving asshole who had been caught doing things he shouldn't have while on duty. Instead of firing him, the brass made him a snitch, and one of his assignments was the bachelor party. This cop was so low that he once took a police car to a city park and dug up plants and trees for his new house. He also stopped an owner of a paint factory for speeding and then told the guy he would tear up the ticket after telling him, "I just built a new home, and could sure use paint to finish it." I even heard later when I was working undercover in narcotics that this cop was acting as an enforcer for some drug dealers. According to my source, the sleaze would sit in uniform during drug transactions to scare off any trouble.

I was asked what my part was in the bachelor party, and I answered truthfully, "I was drunk and didn't see a damn thing. There were too many people in the way."

I was told, "Take five days off without pay, and here is your copy of the pinky."

Oh, good. I think I now have an even half-dozen.

They couldn't get most of us for anything other than "Conduct Unbecoming a Police Officer."

I don't remember the total on how many guys got time off. It was probably around twenty-five. A few cops even got fired.

The cop whose bachelor party it was, got fired.

The cop, who drove his police car in uniform to pick up the

dirty movies, got fired. The cop who escorted the strippers to the party got fired. The guy who collected the money for the hookers (strippers) got fired. It was a real blood bath. My poor partner Bobby, got called in, and was told, “Take five days off without pay for being at the party.”
Bob said he wasn’t there; he was at his dad’s retirement party all night.
The captain interviewing Bob said, “You had to be at the bachelor party. Lazares was there. You two do everything together.”
They did some more checking and then let Bobby off the hook. I later appealed my case and got my five days pay back.

Bob and I were working the far west side of Tacoma one night when we got a call about a domestic with shots fired. Family fights are bad enough, but when guns are involved it can get really hairy. We drove into the neighborhood and parked several houses away. We were told to wait for Sgt. Raymond, and that the wife involved was in a house across the street from the residence we were going to. We contacted the woman and she informed us that her husband had beaten her, and then got a gun and was going to shoot her. She grabbed a rifle and shot at him, and then ran out of the house. She said her husband was still inside somewhere and he had the rifle and other guns.

Sgt. Raymond called the house a couple of times but he got no answer. The house was a single floor over a daylight basement. The front of the house was street level, but the back was two stories high. The drapes were all pulled and we could not see into the house. So Raymond decided we would enter the basement, climb the stairs leading to the main house, and then try and talk to the husband. We stacked in the basement with Raymond leading the way. I was next and Bob was last. There were no lights and we were crowded into that narrow stairwell. My mind was really starting to play tricks with me, and I could swear I heard the husband moving about upstairs. We finally reached the main floor and Raymond started turning the knob on the door. As he eased it open, we were all pointing guns in different directions. I was certain I was going to see a gun come poking around the corner, and there was no way anyone could miss shooting us.

I looked down and spotted a blood trail going from the kitchen on our left down a hall, where it stopped at a closed door on our right. We were all looking at it, but you couldn't tell if it started in the kitchen or ended there. We spilled out into the hallway and Raymond went right, as I went left toward the kitchen. A few seconds later, sarge yelled it was all clear. The husband, after being shot in the kitchen, drug himself down the hall into the bedroom, closed the door, and died. The wife had nailed him with one shot from the rifle, and blew a hole big enough in his chest to put your fist through. Weaker sex my ass.

A few nights later we got a similar call about another domestic with a shooting involved. We arrived at a house just off Portland Ave. near the Indian reservation. The fire department and medics were already there, and when we entered, we found them working on a guy in the bedroom. The victim was buck naked, and part of his right ass cheek and a large chunk of thigh were blown off. He was alive but in a lot of pain. The shooter was identified as the victim's wife, so we took her into the living room to interview her. The wife looked a lot like a punching bag.

She said: “My husband is a karate expert, and when he is drunk he comes home and uses me for practice. Tonight he was punching me when he decided it was time to just kill me. We were in the bedroom. He got out a shotgun and loaded it, looked at me, and told me he didn’t want to get blood on his clothes. He leaned the shotgun up against the dresser, and took off his shoes, socks, and shirt. He then undid his pants and dropped them down over his feet. When he bent over to take them off, I figured this was my chance. I grabbed the shotgun and blew his miserable ass off.”

Lady, I don’t think there is a jury who will convict you.

Not all domestics ended up with shots fired. Sometimes it would just take a good dose of water to cool things off. Bobby and I got dispatched to the Washington State Patrol Headquarters which was just off 38th and South Tacoma Way. When we arrived, we were met by WSP Troopers who informed us that they had a couple in their office who were fighting, but were now separated. We took “Mr. and Mrs. Domestic” out to our car and put them both in the back seat. We started interviewing them, but it was difficult because of two factors.

One. The husband would not shut up and kept provoking his wife.
Two. It was pouring down rain and neither one of us wanted to stand outside with a spouse. The WSP had already made it clear that we were not welcome back in their building with the squabbling couple.

I finally had it up to my neck tie if I had had one on. I yanked open the back door and drug the husband out of the seat. I then handcuffed him to the outside front passenger door handle. I got back into the car and closed the door.

Up to this point, the entire front of the WSP offices had the window blinds open and there was a trooper in each office watching us. As soon as I stuck the husband outside in the downpour, handcuffed to the door, all the window shades went down. I joined back in with the interview of the wife until I heard a gentle knocking on my window. I looked up at the drowned rat that was standing there, and rolled my window down a couple of inches. "Mr. Rat" quietly informed me that he was sorry and if I would let him back in the car, he would behave. We shortly let the two love birds be on their way home.

ELECTRA GLIDE IN BLUE

Bobby and I, plus our wives and kids, were attending the annual TPD Christmas party in 1972 when we spotted Lieutenant McConnell sitting by himself. McConnell was at that time in charge of a new traffic unit that was starting up called S.T.E.P. This stood for "Selective Traffic Enforcement Program", and there would be about nine people assigned to S.T.E.P. The unit had four traffic cars and four motorcycles plus a sergeant. Bob and I did what any self respecting adult would do. We got down on the floor and licked McConnell's feet, while begging and sniveling. We left that night with a promise to be considered for the motorcycles. Hot damn!

A few days later, we got called in from patrol and told we were being transferred to S.T.E.P, and to report to the Traffic Division. On January 2nd, Bob and I showed up and found our new partners, Mike Moorhead and Jim Jensen. Moorhead had ridden bikes in the traffic unit, and was going to be our instructor. The four of us were issued new Harley Davidson police bikes. Now we just had to buy or scrounge boots and a leather jacket. Guys were always coming and going from the motorcycle unit, so finding a jacket for sale was not a problem. As for boots, there was a police uniform supply store in Seattle that carried these really nice slip-on boots that came all the way up to your knees. We scheduled a road trip because I had to have a pair of those boots!

By the following Monday we had the bikes all ready, and each of us had gone to the supply room and obtained a helmet and rain gear. If you ride a motorcycle in Washington State, you had better have rain gear.

The four of us would be heading out each day and to learn maneuvers that would keep us safe. We learned high speed chase techniques, and how to turn around going uphill and down. We were taught how to ride in two and four man formations, and how to pick up a bike that was down. The most important lesson was on how to walk into a restaurant or bar looking very cool. I had my tall shiny boots, black gloves, and leather jacket, white scarf, sunglasses, and a big iron on my hip.

There was never a motor officer who didn't think he was the greatest thing since sliced bread.

During our training, poor Jensen took more spills than anyone should ever have to. But they were not his fault. Of the four Harleys, he got “the lemon.” For some reason, about once a day or sometimes more, the transmission would lock and send him sailing ass over handlebars. The Harley shop worked on this bike continually, but couldn’t find the gremlin. Eventually Jensen would give up the bike and take over a traffic car. It would have made anyone nervous waiting for the next seizure and crash.

The duty of STEP was to be assigned to work areas of the city with high incidence of accidents. One day you would work an area and write a ticket to everyone who violated the traffic laws. The next day you would be assigned an intersection or stretch of road and sit out where everyone could see you. The idea was not to write any tickets, but see if just being visible would cut down on violations. It was not much in the way of police work and was usually pretty boring after coming off 4th Relief, but I was a motorcycle cop and having more cop fun.

I was also riding funeral escorts at this time for a private company owned by another police officer. Each of us had our own bike assigned to us and kept them at home. These were used Tacoma PD bikes. They were stripped down older models, and most had to be kick started. The STEP bikes were kept at the police station, so I would ride either my escort bike or my chopper to work, and then ride the department bike all day. Life was good - funeral escort wasn't. I was just too dumb to know what risks were involved with doing escorts.

Depending on the size of the funeral, I may be working alone or I could have two or three bikes helping. If I was working alone, once the procession started it was my job to lead the funeral through an intersection while I held traffic at a stop. Then when the last car went through I would roar back alongside the procession either on the left forcing oncoming cars over, or on the right and go to the next intersection.

If there were two or more bikes, I would keep leapfrogging until the procession arrived at the cemetery. All of this was done while straddling an ancient kick start Harley and making $11.00 a ride. There was a high turnover in escort duty. Guys would either finally have enough scares, or were tired of kicking that bike only to not have it start when you needed it. I dealt with rain, snow, hail, and cars turning in front of me. Or guys just crashed.

I got called to a funeral one day, and by the time I got to the funeral home, it was snowing. When we got ready to head for the cemetery there were about six inches of snow on the ground. I rode in first gear all the way with both feet on the ground acting as outriggers. There were three of us when we started that escort. The other two crashed and ended up injured. I finished alone and quit after that funeral. I figured I had done enough scary shit in my lifetime.

Each of us was quietly given a key to the Harley shop, which at that time was on the corner of East 25th just off Pacific Ave. You never knew when something might break on the bike, and rather than explain it to your sergeant, you just went down to the shop and fixed it yourself. They also had a refrigerator and there might be a beer or two in it. Some of the things we were forbidden from doing were also the things we loved to do. The boss was always concerned we were going to damage the bikes, and rightly so! Entering or leaving the back of the police department necessitated going as fast as you could and then doing high speed turns. That way you could get the bike way over on its side and scrape the floor boards. It was necessary to make a lower turn than your partner, and if there were just "regular policemen" standing around, you had to show off for them. This made noise and this made sparks, and this made pissed off bosses.

"God damn it! Stop doing that!"

"I didn't do it sergeant! It must have been that asshole Yerbury!"

Then they would go out to look at my bike and find all the paint and some metal scraped off the frame under the floor boards.

It was also a lot of fun to fly down the hills of Tacoma, shut off the ignition, roll the throttle a couple of times to load up the cylinders with gas, then turn the ignition back on. The resulting back fire would scare the crap out of the citizens. It also caused the mufflers to explode occasionally. Then it was another trip to the Harley shop for repairs.

Motor officers were a little different from other cops. You had to be a bit crazy to ride those things in traffic at high speed. Not to mention that if you had been drinking after work, you might just fail to make a turn and end up lying on somebody's lawn. Those big old Harley police bikes were wonderful for making the shopping trips to 7/11 stores. If you didn't carry a bunch of crap in your saddle bags like ticket books and extra clothes, you could fit a bag of ice and a twelve pack of beer into them.

"Hello! Police department. How can I help you?"

"You can come out here and get this policeman and his motorcycle out of my petunias."

The sergeant would round up a couple of volunteers to retrieve the bike and drive the officer home. No one ever said anything to the brass and everyone took care of each other.

Then there were the "wings." This was a pair of aviator wings which were worn upside down by whichever officer "last crashed his bike." If you went down and it was discovered, the guy with the wings would rush to your side and pin them on. Even if you happened to be in surgery getting a broken part fixed. This was another reason for having a key to the Harley shop.

"If you went down and no one saw it, did a Harley really fall in the forest?"

I remember one motor officer coming out of surgery and the only part not bandaged was his ass. So that is where the "wings of dishonor" were placed.

I was working "speeders" out near the mall one afternoon when a car went sailing by. I clocked him at Mach 2 in a 35 mph zone and then pulled him over to issue a ticket. I went up to get his driver's license, and then went back to the bike to run his name. Dispatch came back a short time later and told me the guy was wanted on a felony warrant. I asked for a backup car for transport and then walked back to the driver's window. I told this guy he was under arrest and to step out of the car. The door opened up and out came this guy, and he kept on coming! The next thing I know I was staring at his belt buckle.

This guy went about 6 feet 5 inches, and weighed about 300 pounds. I was thinking Oh Shit! I told him to walk to the trunk and put his hands on the lid, step back and spread his legs. He did everything I asked of him. I patted him down and then went to handcuff him. He volunteered to do it himself and even read his own rights. A patrol unit showed up and I stuffed this guy in the rear seat. I followed them down to the station, and when we arrived I took custody and escorted him into the station. I walked him into the elevator for the ride to the jail and he moved as far from me as he could get. I was really thinking that this is all kind of strange, but I didn't know why. I got him out of the elevator and through the sally port to the booking desk. The sally port was a secure area where we checked our guns into keyed lockers before entering the physical jail. There were now about a half dozen cops and jailers standing around looking at this giant. I un-cuffed him, and he gave out this really big sigh. I couldn't stand it anymore and I had to ask him what is going on and why is he so docile.

He said, "You don't remember me do you?"

I told him no.

He replied, "A year or so ago I was being chased by a bunch of cops and I T-boned your police car. I was afraid you would recognize me and beat me up. I figured once I was in the jail I was safe."

This guy had six-inches on me and over a hundred pounds, and he was worried! Until I got him behind bars I kept thinking, "I hope he doesn't decide to resist, I don't have enough bullets in my gun."

I had decided, or it was decided for me, that I should get my package clipped. I had three kids and Heleen and I decided we didn't need four. It's time for a vasectomy. I had about two weeks to make sure I was going through with it, or to back out of the operation. I talked to my brother-in-law who had also decided to have it done. He was scheduled before me and I wanted to know what to expect. He said that his doctor is an innovator and I should use him. He told me, "My doctor didn't know how to do vasectomies, so he sat down on his couch in front of the T.V and had a few drinks. He then dropped his pants, administered some more anesthesia with a well placed shot, and clipped his own tubes. Anyone who can do their own, can sure as hell do mine."

A few days later I got a call from the brother-in-law, and he told me that my other brother-in-law went with him for the appointment as moral support. They were in the waiting room when the doctor came out and said to them: "Well, as long as you are both here, how about we do a two for one special?" With that they both went in lay on adjacent tables and got themselves snipped. A twofer.

I called my doctor's office and told them I was ready. They instructed me to take a shower before coming in and that I needed the area shaved. This could either be done at home, or by the nurse in the office.

"Do you have a cute nurse or is it the one with the mustache? I think maybe I'll handle that chore."

They were not specific about just what was to be shaved so I erred on the side of "Cleanliness is next to Godliness," and shaved everything from my navel to my knees. I was standing in the bathroom and this area felt kind of tender, so I grabbed a hand full of aftershave and rubbed in on.
Oh my God! Did that ever burn? I had tears streaming down my face.

I screamed like I just had a hot poker rammed up my ass, and then I was on my tip toes trying to wash everything off in the sink. I didn't quite dangle far enough to run my privates under the faucet, so I'm throwing water on myself the best I can. Heleen was beating on the bathroom door asking if I'm all right and telling me there is a flood of water seeping under the door. I was taking big gasping breaths as I told her I was still alive.

Now it's my turn to be clipped. It's Friday and I got off work, parked the motorcycle, and then drank about eight ounces of Scotch. Heleen drove me to the appointment because I couldn't see straight. It was amazing. I walked into the waiting room and I was instantly sober. I was drunk two minutes ago. My name got called and a nurse took me back to a small room. I got undressed and put on the little gown that allowed your butt to hang out, and then I lay down and waited. The doctor came in and pulled my gown up and then starts laughing. He told me I only had to shave a small spot on each testicle.
"And by the way why is everything all red? You get sunburned?"

He got ready to start and then left the room returning a minute later with Heleen. He told me, "She will be assisting."
He then let her help by holding the body parts as they got cut off. Before you can say, "Sing like the Vienna Boys' Choir," I was out of there with instructions to take it easy. I was also told to bring in a "sample" when I have had twenty ejaculations. "That will be sometime tomorrow afternoon, doc." Ha ha ha.

We got home and I lay in bed with an ice bag snuggled to my crotch. Saturday rolled around, and I was feeling pretty good, and we had a party to attend. So we went out to dinner and drinks, and I even did a little dancing. Sunday showed up and I felt great. Monday arrived and I decide to go back to work. I jumped on the motorcycle and spent the day riding around issuing tickets. Tuesday, Wednesday, Thursday and Friday were spent in bed with swollen nuts and multiple ice packs. Macho my ass.

"All units - Report of an armed robbery - Suspects are four black females in a white Ford convertible - Last seen in the vicinity of 9th and K Street southbound."

I was sitting on my bike at 15th and Tacoma Ave watching the intersection. I raced up the hill to K St. which was one way going southbound. I drove up on the sidewalk and headed north. At the corner of 13th, I spotted the suspects' car and pulled them over at gunpoint. I just slammed to a stop in front of them, pulled my gun and aimed at the driver. She got the message. Immediately there were a bunch of police cars arriving, and we got all the suspects out of the car and under arrest. I had four women in dresses and high heels, made up like they were going out on the town. They were separated and brought into the station. As the arresting officer, I got to help with the interviews and do all the paperwork. While they were being interviewed, we discovered that what we had were four prostitutes from Seattle who were supplementing their income by doing armed robberies. We also found out that three of them are ladies and one isn't. It's a "SHIM" (SHE/HIM).

I was in the sergeant's office with several of the brass while they were talking to the woman that wasn't. He informed us that he wants to be a woman and is trapped in a man's body. Someone asked him, "What are you doing about it?"
He replied, "I'm saving all my money for a sex change operation. I have to go to Europe to have it done."
"How much do you need?"
"I think about ten thousand dollars."
"How long have you been saving for the operation?"
"Five years."
"How much do you have saved up?"
"Well, counting today, I have about $125 dollars."
Then our guest told the assembled bosses, "All of this has made me nervous. I have to pee."

The captain looked at the lieutenant, who looked at the sergeant, who looked at the senior patrolman, who looked over at me.
"Lazares, take him to the bathroom."

I didn't want to do this but I had no choice. However I did have a choice where I took him. There were civilian bathrooms, and police bathrooms, and down the hall a bathroom reserved for detectives. I took my prisoner and headed for that one. I walked him in and there was a detective standing at the urinal.
I said, "O.K. Buttercup. Snuggle on up to the trough and let's get this over with."
SHIM says, "I can't pee standing up with this dress and girdle on. I need to sit down."
The detective spun around and peed all down the front of his pant leg while yelling, "What in the hell is going on?"

I took my date to the stalls and told him to get in there and be quick about it. In the next stall over was a pair of shoes with pants bunched around the tops. SHIM steps in and dropped his nylons and panties over his high heels. The next thing that happened was the door to the other stall flew open

and a detective stumbled out holding his newspaper with his pants around his ankles. "What the hell?"
Since they were detectives I thought that they should be able to figure it out.

Bobby was working the intersection of Puyallup Ave and Pacific Ave., and I was up the street at 25th and Pacific. We were on a one hour high profile STEP project. Time was up and we were scheduled to move south on Pacific to another set of intersections. Bob called and told me he is moving south so I can swing in next to him when he passed my location. I heard him coming and started moving to join up. Up the hill on Pacific was a left turn lane for entry onto I-5, and cars were stacked up for about two blocks. There was a pickup trying to get through the stopped cars and get onto Pacific Ave. Someone finally let him through right into our path. I had pulled ahead of Bob to take the lead, and I just missed the truck. Bobby hit it broadside and went down. I spotted all of this in my mirrors and quickly spun around.

Bob was lying in the street, but I saw no blood, and he was moving around. I put out a call of Code 30, and followed that with an announcement, "Officer down at the intersection of 26th and Pacific. I need an ambulance 4 bells and a white car (traffic accident investigation unit)."

I ran up and knelt next to Bobby and found him conscious, but in pain. I immediately asked if I could have his gun and helmet, boots and leather jacket.

He said, "What the hell are you talking about?"

I told him never mind. Then I said, "Don't move, I'll be right back."

I went to my bike and got a piece of chalk and walked back, then started drawing an outline around Bob. He looked at me while I was doing this, and asked, "Why are you chalking my body?"

Bodies only got chalked in fatalities and homicides.

"Ssssh! don't move! Everything will be alright! Can I have your motorcycle and Corvette?"

Cars arrived along with the ambulance. A fellow bike rider announced he was heading our way with the wings. They loaded Bobby in to take him for x-rays and an examination. I jumped on my bike and followed. Every time we stopped at a light, I pulled up next to the rear window and started banging on it. Bobby would look up and I would give him the finger.

At the hospital, I walked in with him when the nurses wheeled him in to the x-ray department. They started stripping Bob, so I started peeling off my gun belt and uniform. The nurse turned around and looked at me then asked, "What the hell are you doing?"

I replied: "Bobby and I do everything together. If he's getting naked for a party, then I'm getting naked for a party."

"Get out of here!"

Bob was banged-up and wouldn't be riding anymore. A couple of days later, I was assigned a new partner, Jim Bass. I was told to break him in slowly, and for the first couple of days just ride around Tacoma so he could get used to the bike. Jimmy and I headed out from the station and worked our way south and east. Eventually I led him onto Pioneer Way East which was a nice two lane road with lots of turns. I was hugging the center lane and Jim was to my right rear. As I went through some turns, I was watching the road and occasionally the mirrors, when I noticed Jim was no longer behind me. I craned my head around, but saw nothing. I quickly made a U-turn and headed back thinking he must have pulled over for some reason. I couldn't find him. I doubled back again and was creeping along when I spotted him lying in the roadside culvert about five feet down. Oh Shit!

"Code 30 - Officer down Pioneer Way East by the fish hatchery - I need and ambulance 4 bells and a white car!"
I've lost two partners in one week. Jimmy ended up with a broken wrist and a broken ankle. Jim was looking at the scenery and forgot to make a turn. When I got back to the station, I got yelled at by the sergeant, and then the lieutenant, and then the captain. I yelled back. I got blamed for Bobby's wreck.
I said, "Bullshit. How could that be my fault?"
Then I got I blamed for Jim not watching where he was going. Double Bullshit! I may have then mentioned what a bunch of idiots I was working for. I ended up being assigned to the permanent night radar car. No more motorcycle.
I guess I showed them.

I WOULD GET TO HANDCUFF THIS SUSPECT AGAIN

TEN YEARS LATER

PROBABLY THE LAST TIME IN MY CAREER I LOOKED LIKE AN OFFICER

WHY DOES THE CHIEF LOOK AT ME LIKE THAT?

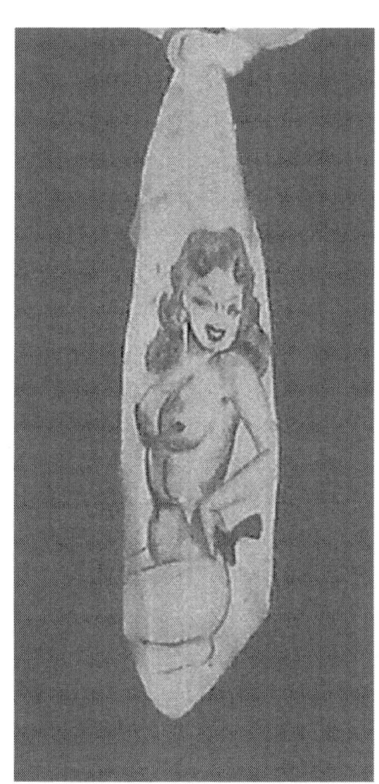

THE TIE

THE TERRIBLE TWO

WHO WOULDN'T SELL DOPE TO ME?

INVESTIGATIONS

I really needed a break. My body was a mess at this point. I had flown helicopters in Viet Nam and managed to touch mother earth abruptly and with force on several occasions. I started my tour of combat at a lofty 6'and due to all the crashes was now down to 5'10". All those compressions shortened me. I crashed or was shot down about eleven times during my two tours of combat, and it had taken a toll.

TPD stuck me on the swing shift radar car and I was not a happy camper or cop. This was my own fault because I couldn't keep my mouth shut. I got in trouble for losing two partners in a one week period on bikes. Instead of just taking the "counseling", I-spouted off and was yanked from the motorcycles. I rebelled the only way I could. I didn't write tickets or I wrote so many I was bound to be the subject of civilian complaints. My "no writing campaign" was merely self-gratification. I was told to get my butt out to certain locations and even though there was no quota, I had better write in excess of twenty tickets each and every shift. I would but each and every one had a big 'W' on it for

"Warning." If I stopped you for speeding you had to be a major asshole to get a written citation that would cost you money. I always set the radar gun for 10 mph over the speed limit, so no one got stopped unless they broke that barrier.

When that program got me yelled at, I went out and set the radar gun for three miles over the limit and wrote so many tickets I was getting carpal tunnel in my right wrist. I think one night I wrote over forty tickets. I was pulling them over three and four at a time and clogging the street with parked cars waiting for their citations.

Pretty soon I was a regular in the captain's office, getting my ass chewed for not writing tickets, or writing too many. Mostly it was my bad attitude more than anything else. Then I destroyed the radar car.

I responded to a large fire in down town Tacoma and was assigned to stop all traffic at the corner of 15th and Pacific Avenue. I was parked crosswise in the intersection so no cars could get past me northbound. I was there for about a half hour, and I needed to change the batteries in my flashlight. I kept spares in the glove compartment, so I opened the driver's side door and leaned in across the seat. I looked up just in time to see a car heading toward me and didn't even have time to brace myself. The car, with one lone occupant, smashed into me doing about 30 miles per hour. I ricocheted off the passenger door and then flew across the seat and exited the driver's door. I found myself lying in the street. I was banged up pretty good, but wasn't bleeding and could walk.

The night "White Car" was requested to do an accident investigation, and I just sat and waited for the outcome. The officer who responded told me that the driver who hit me was an attorney who had been drinking a little. He also told me that the guy was a friend, and could I see my way clear to just ignore everything. I said sure, since I didn't need the hospital and at that time wasn't hurting all that much. I had always managed to bounce back from injuries before. That was the last I heard of the accident investigation, except for getting my ass chewed again for parking the police car in the middle of the street and probably being the cause of the wreck.

Then I destroyed the radar car again.

A few weeks later I was working the radar unit out near 56th and Alaska Street. Dispatch came out over the police radio notifying all units of an armed robbery at a store on 38th and Pine. I responded in that direction just like every other police unit in the south end. I was crossing 45th Street in front of the Tacoma Mall with my lights and siren on. A little old lady, who didn't see me and sure as hell didn't hear me, pulled out right in front of me. I did every evasive maneuver I could think of, but ended up hitting the other car.

I was back in front of the captain again. It was my fault for causing the wreck.

"You had no business running lights and siren to an armed robbery. That is the job of patrol units."

I responded, "I thought it was the job of police officers to try and catch bad guys."

"Well you are not a police officer. You are traffic officer and your job is to write tickets."

After some very careful thought, I formulated what I figured was the perfect answer.

"Take your ticket book and shove it up your ass."

I found myself summoned to the chief's office. I took my customary position in front of his desk, right where the little “x” with my name on it was placed on the carpet. The chief informed me that I had to be more careful with police equipment blah-blah-blah. The chief then told me to stand by the wall while he talked to the captain. The whole thing was out of hand and should never have come this far. So I tuned them out, and turned around to look out the window. The captain came unglued. He started yelling at the chief, that I was insubordinate shitbird, and that I wasn’t even paying attention to him. Well, he had me there! I wasn’t listening to him or caring very much what he said.

The chief then did two things. One was a pinkie, which I had known I was going to get, and the second was a transfer out of traffic and back to patrol.

I had been in the department for three and a half years at this point. TPD came out with a new program called Investigators. There were detectives within the department, but they were detective sergeants. The department needed more detectives, but because of the rank structure, was not going to call them detectives. TPD wanted them all to retire before new detectives were made, so instead, the new rank would be investigator. Investigators would work all shifts, all days of the week. Detectives only worked Monday through Friday 8 a.m. to 4p.m. I signed up, took the written exam, and placed 4th on the list. In March of 1975, I became an investigator. I would be promoted; go to plain clothes with a clothing allowance, and start investigating crimes. I had moved up from patrol to traffic, and back again with a different call sign every time. Now I had a new call sign: "David 17", which I would keep for the rest of my career.

I had to attend the training classes where I learned how to photograph crime scenes and dust for prints. I was then assigned to swing shift patrol units and would be their crime scene investigator. They would call me if they had a burglary, larceny, strong arm robbery, auto theft, or other non-important crimes. The major assaults, armed robberies, and homicides got the detectives called out. I would be doing this for a six month probationary period.

I spent the next 180 days mostly being bored, but there were moments that were cherished. Most of the little investigations have been erased from my mind, but one is clearly etched and will remain for all time.

I got a call to respond to a Laundromat in a little strip mall just east of 38th and Pacific Ave. Two young women were reporting that they had been molested while washing their clothes. I arrived with the intention of dusting for prints all around the business to include the doorway and the machines. While talking to the victims, they told me that they both had been grabbed by the suspect and handled forcefully. I recalled a bulletin that had come out from the chief's office telling everyone in the department that a new technique had been developed where a crime scene technician could lift finger prints from a person's skin. One method was to heat super glue and then blow the fumes onto the skin. When prints developed, they could be photographed. Another method was to brush the area with magnetic powder and again photograph the prints that showed up.

I called the technician and he responded to the Laundromat. The two of us took the first girl into a small office and explained that the technician would be able to dust her skin and hopefully find the suspect's prints. I then asked the girl to show where the suspect had grabbed her. She indicated her left arm and the tech started brushing the area with powder. Nothing appeared, so I asked her to show me another area that the crook grabbed. With that she reached down and took hold of her shirt bottom and pulled it over her head. She was bra-less and pointed to her left breast. I immediately volunteered to do the dusting. The tech shoved me out of the way and told me, "No one but me touches my magnetic powder."

I said, "Nobody move. I'm going to the car and get my camera."

A long time later, we took the second girl into the room and again went through our spiel about the fingerprints. This girl jumped out of her chair and started unsnapping her pants. I told the tech, "You are on your own. I'm going to go fight crime."

Then my probation period came to a climatic end.

I reached my last day working as a probationary investigator, and I planned to celebrate. A friend of mine who worked for another police department asked to ride along on this special day, and we both got dressed-up so we could hit a bar or two after my shift ended at 10 p.m. I was wearing nice tan corduroy pants, and a printed silk shirt.

I had on a "Members Only" jacket that concealed my gun and handcuffs. I was styling!

The night was pretty uneventful and I eventually worked my way downtown to see if I could scare up some action. It was about 8 p.m. and I was driving down Commerce St. nearing the intersection of 13th. I looked over to the sidewalk and spotted a young girl with blood running down her face. Her clothing was torn and she looked a mess. I double parked and walked over to find out what had happened to her. She said she had been hitchhiking around 72nd and South Tacoma Way when a man offered her a ride. Once inside the car, he began hitting her and then sexually assaulted her. When he was finished, he drove downtown and threw her out of the car. She said she watched him park and walk into a business, then she began looking for a cop.

I asked her where the business was and she said down on Pacific Ave. I put her into the back seat of my investigator's car and drove down to Pacific Ave. She finally pointed to a porn theatre near the corner of 15th Street. I pulled to the curb and got a description of the suspect from my victim. I told her that I was going into the theatre to see if I could spot him and make sure he was still inside. If he was, I was going to call for backup and arrest him.

I walked into the lobby of the theatre and came face-to-face with the suspect. He was on his way out. He took one look at me, knew I was the police, and jumped me. The fight was on, and we punched and hit each other as we banged all over the lobby. I eventually knocked him to the floor. The manager of the porn palace was staring out the ticket window, and I yelled, “Call the cops!”

I was now on top of this dirt bag, and he had both hands on my pistol, trying to pull it from my holster. I had one hand on my gun trying to keep it under my control and one hand on the crook to keep him pinned down. My mind was racing and I was thinking about stories I had heard about cops losing their guns to the bad guys and getting shot. Now I was thinking the same thing was going to happen to me. I let go of his throat and pulled my flashlight from my rear pocket. I started hitting the crook in the head as fast and as often as I possibly could. A thirteen-year old boy doesn’t take this many strokes. I finally knocked him unconscious, rolled him over, and handcuffed him. I then dragged him out the door and threw him on the sidewalk next to my car. I called for help and lay down next to the asshole because I was too tired to stand up.

Patrol units arrived and took the guy to the hospital where he received about 100 stitches to his face and head. I took the victim into the station for photographs and a statement. Then I waited for my suspect so I could book him. I talked to dispatch to find out if they got a call from the porn theatre, and they said they did. The manager told them a vice cop was wrestling on the floor with someone. Dispatch called the vice guys who were working somewhere else. They said that they were all together and none of them were involved in a fight. Dispatch then just put out a routine call for any unit to swing by the porn theatre and see about a fight.

It was now 11 p.m., and I was officially off duty and off probation. My police friend asked if I still wanted to go hit a bar and I said, “Hell yes!” He then asked if I had looked at myself. My silk shirt was ripped and covered with blood. My tan cords were covered in blood from the waist to the cuffs, and they would later be thrown away along with the shirt. My hands were cut and bloody, and my face had scratches and was swollen.

I said, “The place we’re going, we’ll fit right in. No one will even give us a second look.”

We drove downtown to a place called O’Brien’s, walked in and up to the bar. Everyone just stared at me and moved away. We had one whole end of the bar to ourselves.

I got pulled in from street duty soon after and was assigned to the Crimes Against Property Unit. This group of investigators and detectives worked burglaries, larcenies, check cases, fraud, and anything else not dealing with Crimes Against Persons.

I immediately drove downtown to the police clothing and equipment shop. I purchased a badge holder for my belt and a shoulder holster for my service revolver. Then I made a quick trip to the Goodwill store where I picked up a used, tan trench coat. I now looked the part. Or at least looked like a kid trying for the lead in “Colombo.”

Being the rookie I got stuck on the “Theft of Garbage Cans” desk and the first case I got was about six missing garbage can lids from the south end. New guys got assigned to easy crimes so that they learned the ropes. I should have been able to solve this quickly. I just needed to arrest my old partner Bobby, but then he would have ratted me out and I would have had to book myself.

Over the course of the next few months, guys moved in and guys moved out. People moved up and others moved down. It was never static except for those who were very content to do little and just wait out their time until retirement. They would in the following order, spend their day.

Arrive at fifteen seconds to 8 a.m.

Drink coffee and read the paper until it was time to go to the bathroom.

Leave with all of the other detectives and go to breakfast.

Come back to the station to use the bathroom again.

Go to lunch.

Come back to the station to use the bathroom again.

Call people. This was usually a wife or girlfriend, but not at the same time.

Go to the bathroom.

Watch the clock from 3 p.m. to 4 p.m.

Try not be the last one out the door.

As a matter of fact, about half the office looked like an assisted living facility.

Bob got promoted, spent his time in patrol as an investigator, and then moved into the Crimes Against Property Unit. The unit also got a few other new guys who had just gotten promoted. We had one other new investigator who was spending more time looking up the dress of a waitress at Denny's than looking for crooks. He was married. She was married. Just not to each other. I started hearing stories that the gal's husband was looking for the unknown investigator, with the intention of shooting him. There were about a dozen of us with desks lined against the windows looking out onto the back parking lot of the station. I for one didn't want to be mistaken for the "Dick" who was slipping the "dick" to the waitress, and end up shot.

One morning Bobby, another investigator, and I, came in early. We moved our desks as far as possible from the hunted one's desk, and then we went outside and taped up giant arrows pointing to the desk of the philanderer. If the husband was a sniper, we wanted to make sure he knew who to shoot. Then a large bull's eye was taped over the investigators window. He didn't think we were funny, but he did ask for a different desk somewhere in the basement.

Crimes Against Property was a training ground for all the new investigators. The cases were varied and although most were routine, there was always something to be learned from them. I ended up on a few cases arresting guys I had gone to high school with. They were the ones who never had anything to do with me because I wasn't cool enough, tall enough, smart enough, or had a car. Well, I got a car now and it has lights and a siren!

"Hi - remember me? - No? Doesn't matter - Put your hands on the wall - Feet back and spread 'em! Let me hold your letterman's jacket for you. I'm sorry - handcuffs too tight?"

I also arrested about a half dozen old girlfriends. They were not aware that they had been my girlfriend, but as I read them their rights, I made sure to tell them how I had broken up with them, and I was sorry. High school couldn't have been pleasant for them not dating me.

"Hi. Aren't you Michael from my high school class?"
"Why yes, I am."
"What are you doing now Michael?"

"I'm a Proctologist."
"Oh my gosh. You're a doctor!"
"Not exactly. I just spend all of my time dealing with assholes."

I joined a slow pitch softball team with some other guys in the office including, O'Malley. We also had some civilians on the team because I think they all worked for our team sponsor, so we might as well let them play. Our unofficial sponsor was Dean's Tavern on 38th street. We spent every night after practice there, and of course we celebrated our wins and losses in the bar.

I showed up after a game with the crotch split out of my pants. I was my usual commando and in danger of dropping the family jewels into the pitcher of beer. Team mate Kenny's wife decided it was her duty to render aid, so I got hoisted onto the pool table and she performed surgery on the rip. I mean, what woman doesn't carry a complete sewing kit in her purse. I'm trying not to let her immediate proximity cause a swelling, because her husband is standing right next to me holding a pool cue. I also don't want to make the lady nervous, and end up with my pants sewn to my wee wee. Thank the lord Heleen was also there, as I never would have been able to explain this.

Another night after a game and we had been in the bar for a while and had way too much beer. O'Malley slid up next to me and said, "See that guy at the end of the bar? I know him and I am positive he is wanted on a felony. Keep an eye on him, and I'll call the station and confirm the warrant." Pat then went to the pay phone in the back of the bar and called in.

Meanwhile, as Pat waited for confirmation, the crook slid off his bar stool and headed out the front door. Pat came back a minute later and says, "Yup, the asshole is wanted for felony narcotics. Which way did he go?" I pointed, and we ran out the door in our baseball uniforms and jumped in Pat's van. This was your standard, "I've got kids" van with the sliding door on the passenger side. We drove about a block and spotted the doper in a phone booth on the corner of 38th and Yakima at the Jubilee Drive-in. We pulled into the parking lot, bailed out, ran up to the phone booth, and yanked the door open. "Mr. Wanted" starts yelling into the phone that he is being kidnapped as we jerked him out and threw him up against the van. I patted him down while Pat called the station to get us a police car for transportation. No cars were available, so we grabbed the crook and threw him into the van and told him, "Lie on the floor and don't move." I got back into the front seat and O'Malley got behind the steering wheel, and we informed our arrestee that we were taking him to jail.

I opened the glove box and took out a pint of whiskey. I helped myself and then passed the bottle to Pat. The crook was crying and whining about going to jail, so Pat passed the booze to him. The three of us sat there and drank the pint. Finally a patrol car showed up and the two officers are staring at us, wondering why in the hell they got this call.

Here are two drunken detectives with no guns, badges or handcuffs, wearing baseball uniforms, drinking with a wanted felon, who they have arrested in a phone booth. *"Hi guys. Would you mind taking this shithead to jail and maybe writing up the arrest report? We really need to get back to the tavern where we left our beer, wives and team mates.*

O'Malley and I received another accolade when we solved a string of burglaries and arrested the two pukes who were responsible. Pat knew a lot of crooks because he was related to one, and through him he met a whole bunch of dopers. These particular crooks were using vice grips to twist off door knobs to gain entry to homes.

A report came in that a homeowner in Lakewood came back to his residence and found two people burglarizing it. He was threatened with a crowbar by a big Indian and his smaller white partner. Pat heard the description and immediately knew who the guilty parties were. The two made their getaway in a VW bug and the victim got the license plate number. The car came back registered to a known felon who lived in the 3700 block of Tacoma Ave. South. Pat went by and found the car parked in the alley and called for assistance. I showed up along with some patrolmen. We kicked in the front door, entered and after a foot race through the house, we arrested "Tommy Tennis Shoes" and "Eugene the Indian." These arrests led to others, and the entire crew of burglars was soon awaiting trial. Neither Pat nor I even had to use a phone booth.

KIDDY KOP

I was notified that I was being transferred to the Juvenile Unit. This group dealt with "kiddy crime." If they were under 18 years of age, and doing bad things, we had to deal with them. It was mostly youngsters doing burglaries, car thefts, vandalism, and other assorted mischief. I didn't like my time in "Juvie", but had a great boss in Lieutenant Bob Baldassin (aka: Baldy). My problem was that I was Baldy's problem. I didn't break the rules so much as bend the hell out of them a time or two. Baldy would give me a half-hearted ass chewing and tell me to sin no more. Then he would shove me out the door to go fight crime.

One prime example was when I was assigned to a bunch of burglaries that were taking place near 84th and Yakima. These were all done during the daytime and probably the work of students from Baker Jr. High school. I visited the school and got a list of kids who were absent on the days of the break-ins, and then started doing interviews. It was not difficult to find one of the guilty parties, and get him to rat-out the others in the group. When I had finally arrested everyone, it was time to get a search warrant and round up all the property they had stolen. I got the paddy wagon from the station and visited the kids' houses and then transported everything to the police station. Then it was time to match the stolen swag with the reported items taken and call the victims. I had several items that were not on any reports so I loaded up two of the criminals, and had them show me houses they had broken into.

As I made the rounds I was shown one house that I knew. It belonged to an Attorney in Tacoma, who was, at the time, a partner of my brother, Danny. I asked the kids what they had taken from that particular house and they told me, "We got a TV, a gun, some jewelry, and a blow-up doll that's naked." I asked where the doll was and they informed me they had given it to someone else. I tracked it down and confiscated it and then returned to the station. I found the reported burglary and looked at the property listed. TV, jewelry, gun. No doll. I called the Attorney and we chit-chatted, and I informed him that I had made an arrest and had all his stolen stuff and he could come down and identify it and pick it up. I also asked, "Was there anything else stolen that he now remembered?"

He said, “Nope.”
I called my brother, filled him in, and swore him to secrecy. I then met with him at their law office after they closed for the day. The doll got inflated, and was then seated in the partner's chair behind his desk. We turned off the lights and departed.

The next morning I heard that the secretary came in first to make coffee and open the office up for business. She entered the attorney’s office, spotted my little present, and quickly locked the office door. It didn’t take too long before Baldy got a call threatening the police department, his and my life, and anyone else who might have been involved. Of course Baldy had to find out about the outrage, and was looking high and low for me. I called my brother, who called his partner, and explained that it was all a little joke.

The partner was laughing his ass off and said, “I know it was. It was funny as hell and you almost gave my secretary a heart attack. She thought I was having an affair with vinyl. I only called TPD so I could yank your brother’s chain.”

Bob Baldassin sat next to my desk in the Juvenile office. I think he did this on purpose. He was hoping that my skills as a detective would rub off on him. I know for a fact that Baldy was a great administrator, but he could not sleuth his way out of a rest room.

Case in point. Baldy got his butt gnawed off by “Mrs. Baldy” for smoking, so he had to quit. However, he took up chewing tobacco, but only in the office where she couldn’t catch him. Since we shared floor space, Baldy would spit in my trash can rather than messing up his own. That way he also could claim that I was the one chewing if someone was to check. I kept yelling at him and threatening him if he didn’t quit spitting in my trash can. All to no avail.

One day I drove to my mother-in-law’s house and helped myself to a can of cayenne pepper. I went back to the station at lunch time when no one was around. I got out the little can of chew Baldy always kept it in his top, middle drawer. I poured the pepper into the can and stirred it up so you couldn’t see it, then I left the station. I came back at around 3 p.m. to do my paperwork, and asked the secretary, “Where is the lieutenant?”

She replied, “Lt. Baldassin came back from lunch and was sitting at his desk. He then started getting really hot and was sweating like crazy. He told me he thought he was getting sick, so he went home.”

Three days later Baldy returned to work, and I had to ask, “I heard you were sick”. He said, “Yes. It must have been the flu. I was nauseous, feverish, and really sweating. I spent three days in bed.”
That was probably the mid 70’s and I still haven’t admitted to him what I did.

Another time, another misadventure, and Baldy was on my case about it. I can’t remember the details, but I’m sure it was trivial. I know it involved some burglaries and property that was cluttering up the office. He told me he wanted the stolen stuff put into evidence or returned to whoever owned it. I wasn’t in the mood for work, but I didn’t mind a little play. Baldy left the office, so I took his swivel chair and left with it for the police garage. When he returned later he found his chair behind his desk as usual, but it now sported a battery pack and a trolling motor that was bolted to the back.

I think he thought it was me, but I couldn't be found and my police radio was not working for some odd reason.

I got selected to go with another detective to arrest some kid who had a warrant for some heinous crime. This Juvie had probably stolen some garbage can lids he found lying around Richburg's house. We arrived at a house up on the hilltop where this guy was living with his grandmother. She brought him to the front door to turn him over to us. I look up and I am staring at this 6' 3" track star. This kid doesn't look like he weighs anywhere close to 150 pounds, and he's wearing "felony high tops." Before I get these thoughts thoroughly processed, the kid jumped off the porch and started "picking-em-up and laying-em-down."

My partner for this simple arrest is old; maybe pushing late 30's and is bigger around than he is tall. I know who has to chase the kiddy crook. I jumped off the porch and began pursuing this budding Olympian and followed him up and down streets, through yards, and over fences. After about a half mile of this, I was dying. I was currently smoking about one to two packs a day and I didn't think they were helping much. We finally went round a house, climbed a fence, and headed for the alley. Just as we got to the garage, I caught this kid when he slipped on some gravel. I couldn't breathe, and I couldn't run one more step. If he decided to fight, he'd kick my ass. I was dead or dying, so I did the only sensible thing. I grabbed the kid by the pants and collar and ran his head into the side of the garage. Boom! This juvenile track star is unconscious, and I'm not far behind. All I can do is lie down in the dirt next to him. A couple of minutes later my temporary partner arrived, and then asked what the hell happened to the kid.

"Did you shoot him?"

I told him after looking for witnesses, "Nope. He was looking back at me instead of where he was going, and ran right into the side of the garage. Damndest thing I ever saw."

I was driving around December 16, 1975 in my underpowered Dodge detective's car, when an "All Units" call came over the police radio. Dispatch was telling everyone that a bank robbery had just been reported at a Commercial Savings and Loan, 317 South 72nd Street. The suspect was a white male, who had pointed a gun at the tellers. I was heading at the bank as I went westbound from Pacific Ave. As I neared the scene, I saw a Thunderbird come from D Street out onto 72nd. The guy driving took one look at me and knew I was a cop. I took one long gander at him and knew from the way he was looking at me, that I was looking at the robber. I hit the lights and siren, informed Tacoma P.D I was in pursuit, and the chase was on.

We were generally heading west and south roaring up and down streets and alleys. I remember going down 72nd then south on Yakima, hitting Park Ave. for a short time and then we were on 84th street still heading in the general direction of S.W. The bank robber was outdistancing me with the Ford. He had a V-8, and I had half that much engine in my little Dodge, but he couldn't lose me.

He then turned left onto Ainsworth and accelerated again. I was trying to chase him, talk on the radio, and keep from wrecking the car. He slid around the corner onto 90th Street and was again heading west. His next turn was northbound on Wilkeson, which was a dead end street. Facing me and the crook was a wooden barricade. He didn't even slow down and plowed straight through it.

He was now on a dirt trail which went up a small hill, down the other side, and then into the trees and brush. As he flew over the hill, his wheels completely left the ground and I expected him to crash as he disappeared over the top. I skidded to a halt and bailed out of the car, and then ran to the top of the hill. The T'bird was sliding sideways but still moving toward the woods. I couldn't think of anything to do because I was all alone and now I didn't have a car. So I opened fire at the crook.

I shot all six bullets I was carrying, and I watched him drive out of sight into the trees without slowing down. This wooded area is about a half mile to a side and contained swamp and trees. As I chased the bank robber, every police officer in the city, Sheriff's deputy and State Patrolman in Pierce County, started to surround the area. Some guys, who were home and off duty were listening to the chase on their police monitors, so they loaded up the deer rifle and headed toward me. *"Honey! Pack me a lunch. I have to go to Tacoma and shoot an asshole."*

I had cops everywhere all wanting to get a piece of the bank robber. I went from cop to cop and car to car begging for someone to give me bullets.

"Nope! Sorry! You used all of yours and you can't have mine!"

Finally, one of my co-workers gave me six rounds of his, but told me not to shoot them as he wanted them back.

The bank robber's car was finally spotted behind a very large cottonwood tree south of a church on 84th Street. Everyone started moving in that direction when a single gunshot sounded. We all cautiously closed-in on the tree and found the bank robber lying behind it with a self-inflicted gunshot wound to his head. It was later determined that this crook was an escapee from a prison in Ohio, where he was doing time for killing a cop. I was kidded unmercifully for running out of bullets and causing a suicide. The police department gave me an award for heroism, but nobody mentioned that part.

NARCS

I had been whining and crying to anyone who would listen and it finally paid off. I had orders assigning me to the Narcotics Unit. I was to report the first of January 1976. I think part of it was because of the bank robber incident. I immediately quit shaving and getting my hair cut. Then I went shopping for every t-shirt I could find which said anything remotely like: "Grass, weed, high, coke, coca cola, or H." I bought a few, and although I thought I was now cool and looking the part, I only looked like a detective, new to the narcotics unit who had bought himself a bunch of dumb t-shirts.

I began my training as a narcotics officer and was assigned different partners to get an idea how they worked and to learn the ropes. Some guys were real "go getters" who spared no time or effort to chase dopers. Other detectives didn't do much except rely on their snitches for information. Some just sat around waiting for the phone to ring. It wasn't unusual for someone to call in to rat-out their friends and neighbors. It may be revenge or something as simple as getting rid of a competitor. *"Hey Officer! If you hurry to the corner of 23rd and K Street, Smiley is dealing heroin. He has some in his right sock. Don't tell him I called!"*

"How can I do that? I don't know who I'm talking to."

"Duh! Okay. Don't tell him it was me, Calvin. How long before that corner be opening up?"

One of my first assignments was to help-out vice. They had a house near 73rd and Yakima under surveillance that was being used for illegal gambling, prostitution, and maybe drugs. I was a new face, so it was decided to send me into the house with an informant who would introduce me and get me into the poker game. The plan was laid out so that once I was sitting at the table, my snitch would lose his money and leave. That way when the bust went down later they would maybe not remember who brought me into the house.

The two of us arrived around 8 p.m. and I was invited to sit down at the table. I looked up and sitting across from me is a childhood friend, Skip, who was the son of the owner of Brown's Star Grill. His eyes were all bugged-out of his head because he knew I was a cop. Before he can say a word I kicked him under the table then stuck my hand across the table and introduce myself as ‘Doc’. He didn’t know what to do, but he caught on quick and just shut up.

I played poker and kept track of all the money the house was raking out of the pot. Everyone would ante and the guy running the game would take” the house cut” out of the pot. I was also watching two women who were serving drinks and hanging around. They sure looked like hookers that I had seen before, but no one was currently interested in them. The poker game went on for a couple of hours, then it was time for the arrest team to hit the front door. Just prior to the bust going down, I told Skip I wanted to talk to him about a private matter. No one questioned this, so I took Skip into the bathroom, told him what was going to go down, and then I shoved him out the window. It was the least I could do for him not ratting me out.

This case was being run by the State of Washington Gambling Commission and they had a couple of officers assigned. Our vice unit and a couple of patrol units, who were assisting, all hit the front door and arrested everyone in the house. I got handcuffed, thrown in the back of a police car and taken to the station. That way they wouldn’t know I was a cop until the trial, and hopefully not connect me with the informant. Once everyone was segregated, I was placed into an office by myself to write the reports and identify all the evidence.

There was a lady selling heroin out of a house on Portland Ave near 62nd street. A couple of narc officers had tried several times to catch her with drugs, but were not having any luck. They were using an informant who was buying from her, and then they would draw up a search warrant and hit the house. Finally, the informant told them that she was flushing the drugs down the toilet. This was usually bad because the drugs would wash right down into the city sewer. But this house hadn't been connected to the sewer yet and was on its own septic system.

Now the Narcs figured they had her. They would serve a search warrant, let her flush, and then open up the septic tank and retrieve the drugs. Another search warrant was served, and this time with a couple of guys along who had to sift the septic tank. Same results. Great plan; shitty execution. The detectives got hold of the snitch in the case and asked what the hell happened this time. He told them that he found out the lady had taken the heroin bags and stuffed them up her vagina because she knew no one wanted to look there.

Another buy and another search warrant, only this time the warrant included a trip to the hospital for a full body cavity check. The door got kicked in and the lady was arrested again and hauled to Tacoma General Hospital. A doctor took her into an examination room, and came out a few minutes later with an evidence bag. Now everyone knew we had her. We just had to bag and tag the dope, and put her butt in jail.
"How many bags of drugs did you find, doctor?"
"None, but I did find a bunch of tiny bones. I think she had a miscarriage at some point, and the fetus just stayed inside her and decayed."
"Say what!"

Nobody knew what to do, so it was decided to send the bones to the coroner's office and then consult with the TPD brass on charges, if any. The next day, the office got called by the coroner who informed the arresting officers that what he had was "chicken bones." The mystery deepened. I could have envisioned just about anything being stuffed inside this woman, but not chicken bones. So began the legend of Chicken Lady" who may have been related to or having relations with "Chicken Man" from my patrol days.

"He's everywhere! He's everywhere!"

I guess including there.

I continued working with different detectives and on occasion with Sergeant Denny. He was a nice enough guy, but I couldn't walk into a convention of blind drug dealers and hope to score. He walked, talked, and dressed police, including the black shined shoes with the cushion soles and white socks. He might as well have just worn a uniform. I was sporting long hair and a beard and ratty clothes. I could walk in somewhere with him and it was always, "Hi Officers!"

One day we were riding down Yakima Ave heading for the station to do our paperwork and finish out the shift. I was driving and he's riding shotgun. I noticed that he was squirming all over the seat. It was like he had a terrible itch on his ass, and he is trying to scratch it on the seat covers. I finally couldn't stand it any longer, and I asked, "What are you doing?"

He replies, “It’s this damn Kotex. I just can’t get comfortable.”

I damn near wrecked the car, while staring open mouthed at Sgt. Denny.

“What Kotex?”

He says, “My hemorrhoids were bleeding this morning and I didn’t want to have blood spots in my underwear. So I used one of my wife’s Kotex.”

I was having a visual and it wasn’t pretty. I would never get that image out of my mind.

The “Kotex Kid” riding to work to fight crime and injustice.

It never stopped with Sergeant Denny. One day we were working together again and I was kidding around with him. He mentioned lunch and I jokingly said I was going home for a “nooner.”

His first question was, “What’s a nooner?”

I told him, and he came right back with, “But it’s still light out”.

I said, “Yes. Usually noon is during the day time.”

He then asked if I had seen my wife naked with the lights on. I’m starting to get a little concerned about the direction of this conversation.

I said, “Yes. I have seen her naked with the lights on.”

He then informed me that he has never seen his wife naked. He told me that she would get undressed in the bathroom or closet then turn out all the lights. She would then slip into bed wearing full-length pajamas.

I had to ask, “If you have never seen her naked, how do you know it’s really her in bed?”

I got back, “You’re right. I’m going to take a flashlight with me next time.”

I started working a lot of undercover operations. I was really looking the part, and I had learned how to make buys. There was no shortage of informants, and the other detectives would set me up with one of their snitches to go in and make a buy. Normally I would get a slight introduction to the crook the first time. Something along the lines of, “That’s Doc sitting in the car.”

I let the dealer get a good look at me. Sometimes this would result in an invite into the house. The next time I went to the house, when a buy was made, I would take the cash out of my pocket and pay the dealer. If they were cool with that, by the third meeting I was making the entire transaction while the informant sat in the car. Then the informant was moved out of the meetings all together. Now the doper is dealing just with me, and they usually would forget who the hell introduced "Doc" when it came time for the arrests. I was pretty much on my own, but would try and have back-up when it was available. I didn't like being in some house by myself, in case the whole thing came crashing down on my head. I knew a lot of people in Tacoma, and I might run into someone I knew in a house. That could get very awkward.

Occasionally, I got payback on the guys who weren't available for surveillance, or who didn't watch my back as close as I felt they should. I started buying dope from this dealer who lived around 36th and Alaska Street. He let me into his house after the third hand-to-hand buy, and I wish he never had. Up to this point all the deals were done through a partially opened door. This guy was raising snakes and lizards. He also had a bunch of mice and rats which he fed to his critters. When I went into his house to do a deal, I would stand in the middle of the living room and keep turning in circles so none of his pets could sneak up on me.

My surveillance team just wasn't covering me like I thought they should. When it came time to arrest the dealer, I did up the search warrant. I gave it to them but it slipped my mind to tell them the house was full of creepy crawlies. Oh Well! They would know soon enough. I was placed on the permanent shit list with those detectives.

On one case, I was introduced to a black heroin junkie who had gotten arrested and was now trying to be a snitch to keep from going to prison. He had one really interesting dealer that he was buying his "H" from. It was a car dealer who also had reputed ties to what passed for the "Mob" in Seattle. The Mafia was not in Washington State as an organization, but they did have people who did business with their blessing. This included strip clubs and drug dealers.

My informant started taking me to the car lot on South Tacoma Way, but I was not allowed inside the office. My snitch would go in with my money, make a buy and come back out to the car. I didn't get to see the transaction, and only had his word that he had bought the drugs from the car dealer. After a couple of weeks and several buys, I was allowed to enter the sales office, but I had to remain in the waiting room. This investigation was not going anywhere fast so I came up with a plan.

I would go to the car dealer on my own and try to make a buy with marked money. A search warrant would be served as soon as I left the building, and the dealer would be arrested. I drew up the plans and told them to the captain who ran our division. He had to okay the plan because I needed a large sum of cash to flash at the buy. I gathered the other detectives, got the search warrant, and then headed out to the car dealership. When I arrived, I was invited right into the office, and was given a seat in front of the crook's desk. He acted like he had never seen me before and asked why I was there. I told him I wanted to score some heroin, and I pulled the cash out of my pocket.

He said: "I don't sell drugs and I don't know anyone who does, and Detective Lazares, I think you are trying to entrap me." I immediately got up and looked behind me to make sure there was no one back there. The hair on my neck was standing on end. I then left the office.

I met with the backup guys and told them what had happened. Every single one of them had been in on this case from the beginning, and any one of them could have ratted me out earlier. Everyone except the captain. Maybe I had just been wearing my badge and name tag this last time, but I thought I knew who may have made the call to the car dealership. This same captain had recently transferred to narcotics from the traffic unit where he had spent several years. He and I had some previous relationships that hadn't gone well.

I had another partner for a while named Stan. Stan was very methodical to the point he didn't put one foot in front of the other without thinking it through. He spent as much time thinking as he could. Stan was like Denny. He wore his police clothes which meant slacks, a sport shirt, and his police shoes with white socks. Stan might as well of worn a sandwich board over his head that said, "Tacoma Police Department. Can you tell?"

But Stan was good at what he did, and what he did was work snitches. People would call in for any number of reasons to inform on drug dealers. Sometimes it was good citizens or neighbors. Other times it was crooks trying to get a deal on an arrest. Or it was dealers trying to eliminate their competition. Whatever the reason, Stan would sign them up and start making controlled buys and writing search warrants.

One night, Stan and I were in the office when the phone rang. The phone was ignored a lot of times at the end of the shift because it always meant more work. When you were looking to get off duty and go home, the last thing you wanted to hear was: "I'm pretty sure my neighbor is smoking dope. Get out here right away and you can catch him."

Stan grabbed the phone and said, "Narcotics."
The voice on the other end of the line said he was watching his neighbor out his back window. The neighbor and two other guys were loading packages into boxes from the trunk of the neighbor's car. He described each package as being about the size of a phone book, wrapped in brown paper, and sealed with tape. Ah Ha!

Before I could register the information, Stan was up and sprinting for the parking lot. I followed and piled into the car with him before he left me standing there. We raced out to N. 30th Street, and after finding the address of the caller, parked down the street and crept into the back yard. We peered through the fence and watched the three suspects holding up packages that looked an awful lot like kilos of marijuana. I figured we would call for backup and then get a search warrant and go in. Not Stan. He raced around the suspect's house, came to a locked gate, and vaulted the six foot high fence. I had never seen Stan hurry to anything other than lunch, and now he looked like superman leaping tall buildings in a single bound. I was ten years younger than Stan, in better shape, and I had to drag my ass over the fence. Stan's feet left the ground on our side and didn't touch anything until he hit the grass on the other side.

By the time I got over the fence, Stan was running up to the garage with his gun out yelling for everyone to freeze. We grabbed the two guys in the garage who were helpers, but the home owner sprinted to his house and locked himself in the basement.

We eventually convinced him to come out and give himself up before we called for assistance and kicked in his doors. We ended up with three arrests, the seizure of a brand new car, and 100 kilos of marijuana. That was a pretty substantial amount of weed in the early 1970's.

There was something going on every single day for the narcotics unit. The biggest focus was on the dope dealers working up on the hilltop. This is where the heroin was being sold and everyone thought that was the scourge that would bring down civilization as we knew it. Cocaine was just coming into vogue, and small time marijuana just didn't get much attention.

A person of great interest was an attorney who was white, but whose clients were black dope dealers. It was rumored that he was trading his time and advice for drugs, and that he really liked coke. We would arrest a dope dealer and before we could get him booked, the attorney was down to get him bailed out. It pissed-us-off, and we started trying to devise ways to arrest the attorney.

One day in court, several of us were sitting there waiting to testify and he was the attorney for the accused. As we watched his performance, we noticed he was slurring his words and was acting like he was drunk or stoned. The court took a break; we all stood up, and this attorney came walking by. I noticed that he had white rings around his nostrils. *"This may be a clue!"* I went up to the prosecuting attorney's office to plead my case for arresting this dirt bag. What I heard was, "What proof do you have? Is there any evidence? How would we convict?"

I tried to convince the prosecutor that we would jump on this attorney in the courtroom and hog tie him. We would then put his head in a plastic bag so we didn't lose any of the evidence. Then we would carry him down to Doc Eagleston in the basement crime lab, and have the barrister analyzed. Doc Eagleston could do this in a heartbeat. No fancy beakers and test tubes for the Doc. No spectrum analysis or chemical tests. Eagleston would simply wet his finger, and stick it into whatever powder you placed in front of him or up an attorney's nostril. He would then ram his finger into his mouth, look at you and say: "Yes. That is coke, or heroin, or meth, or LSD." No wonder the good doctor was usually acting and looking like he was wacked out. The prosecutor put the kibosh on this plan and told me to get out of his office. I went back to the guys, and told them it was a no. We sat and stared holes in the back of the attorney and tried to devise a new plan.

We were always trying to come up with new ways to do surveillance in the area of 23rd and K Street. All the dealers were black and all the narcs were white. We sort of stood-out from each other. We tried to sit in unmarked police cars but that didn't work. Next we tried using a van. Two of us would get in the back and lay down. Then we would be driven to the area, the van would get parked and the driver would get out and walk away. We were in the van about ten minutes when two little kids walked up and started beating on the side of the van.

"Officers! Are you hiding in there? We know you are in there!"

So much for fooling the street-smart kids up on K Street.

After that we hatched the perfect plan. Across the street from the Office Tavern that was a hot bed of illicit dealings, was a storm drain. This was built into the street and had a grate that formed an "L" and was part of the curb. If the right person could be found, and he volunteered, then we would stuff him down the sewer a couple of blocks away. The volunteer would walk in the sewer until he got to 23rd where he would watch the dealers. He would call us on a portable radio to tell us who was selling and we would come flying in and make the arrest. We got no volunteers.

I got called into the office and was told to make myself available to do some drug deals with the DEA (Drug Enforcement Administration). I had an informant who got hooked up with some crooks who were big time dealers. These bad guys wanted to sell in large quantities only! Any dealer who was smart knew that the local cops were limited to how much they could spend. A hundred dollar deal was big time to TPD. If I put together a buy for $500 or $1000, approval had to come down from the chief and the mayor. And I had better not lose the cash. The other side of the coin was the Feds would not do a deal for less than a couple of kilos of coke, or several hundred pounds of grass. All the dealer had to do was sell enough quantity that the local police couldn't afford to make the deal, and a small enough amount that the Fed's were not interested.

For this caper, the informant was going to make the purchase of several kilos of coke, and I was to be the money man. The DEA would provide the money and all of the personnel for the surveillance teams and the arrest teams. An airplane was even brought into the plan to insure that the crooks didn't get away with the money. The snitch would meet with the dealers and inspect the cocaine. If everything was good, he would bring the dealers to me and I would hand them the suitcase full of cash.

I was driven to the parking lot of a restaurant in Puyallup by the informant. He got out of the car and walked a couple of blocks to meet the dealers. Surrounding the area were five teams of DEA on surveillance and two more in a plane overhead. Unknown to me was that the dealers were smarter than the Feds. They had three teams of counter surveillance, and immediately spotted all the narc cars. The DEA didn't want to let me or the money out of their sight, so they were sitting in a circle around me. Every city street around the meeting point had two guys sitting in a car and talking on police radios. A blind man could have found them. Meanwhile I was sitting in the informant's car with a suitcase containing $50,000.

All of a sudden, one of the crooks is standing right next to the car and leaning in the passenger side window. He said to me: "You are a fucking cop, or I'd kill you!"
I was taken completely by surprise and couldn't get to my gun which was in a holster on my ankle.
I stammered, "I don't know what you are talking about! I'm no cop!"

The bad guy was still leaning on the window sill and started telling me about the cars on surveillance and describing the people in them. He then stood back up and ran off behind the restaurant. My great DEA backup is nowhere to be found. Not one of those clowns saw what had happened, and how close I was to losing the money and maybe my life. I got out of the car and stood on the hood, until someone finally spotted me and drove down to see what the hell I was doing. I was so mad I could barely speak. After the debriefing back at TPD, I told my boss I would never work with the DEA again, and I never did.

BATMAN AND ROBIN

STARSKY AND HUTCH

TOODY AND MULDOON

The dynamic duo was back together. Bob got his awaited assignment to Narcotics and was my partner once again. The next couple of years would prove to be some of the craziest I ever had. Most of that was of our own making, and it finally came down to the chief telling us that we were a couple of wacky assholes and that we needed a change of scenery.

Bob and I started working with a few good snitches and we're soon making buys all around the countryside. At any given time, we had four of five people either working off an arrest, or they were connected to the drug scene and wanted to work for the cops. We referred to the snitches as Confidential Informants or C.Is. The two different types of informants created unique problems for us. If the CI was working off a beef, we knew going in that he/she was a crook. They would probably lie to us, or steal drugs if they could. They might try to get away with some of our buy money, and of course continue using drugs. I would give them money for a buy and search them from top to bottom. They had to be completely clean before going into the buy, and they were searched again when they came out to make sure they stayed that way.

"Now let's see. Where did I put those rubber gloves?"

"Here we go." Snap!

"Now bend way over and touch your toes! Wow! You could hide a bale of marijuana in there!"

Once they scored the drugs, they were always either trying to pinch-off a little for themselves or use the drugs while out of our sight. Or they would try and lowball the drug dealer on the original buy price, and then either keep the difference in cash or purchase a little for themselves that they then hid on their person. The CI also continued his life of crime. It wasn't unusual to get a phone call a few times a week from patrolmen or detectives who had arrested your CI.

The CI was told by us that we could and would make little problems go away, but they were on their own if arrested for a felony. Sometimes you just got tired of dealing with the dumb shits. They would get arrested or stopped so many times that I got tired of getting them out of jams.

"Hello Detective! I just stopped this guy for driving a stolen car, and he said to call you. He claims he works for you and that you will help him!"

"Nope! Never heard of him. Lock him up or shoot him. I don't care one way or the other."

The other type of CI was often times even worse. They wanted to be a cop, act like a cop, or just hang around with a cop. It wasn't long into the relationship that the CI started thinking he could run the operation and that you worked for him. This was usually the beginning of the end.

"Hey! It's me Ozzie. I just scored some weed from a guy, and we need to meet so I can give you the dope and get paid back for what I spent."

"No! I have told you one hundred times how this works, and that ain't it. I have to give you marked money and search you. I have to watch you go in and come back out. I have to search you again. What part of that don't you still understand?" "Well I'm out $50 and what do I do with the grass?" "Chalk the $50 up to unsound business practices. If I catch you with the grass, I'll arrest you, and we'll have a brand new relationship."

I tried to use the CI as little as possible. If they could do an introduction to a dealer, great! I would go with them once or twice and then push them out of the buys.

Bobby and I were running all over Pierce County and the greater Tacoma area, buying drugs and arresting people. Earlier in our patrol days street people started calling us Batman and Robin. This reference was to a 1974 movie about two New York cops named Dave Greenberg and Rob Hantz. These two were defying the police brass and making their own rules to arrest crooks. There was a book about them in ‘73 and then the movie.

Now of course that had changed to Starsky and Hutch. These two were TV cops in a fictional California city. Starsky was Blond and Hutch was dark haired. They ran all over the city causing havoc to crooks and dope dealers. Bob was taller, fair skinned and blond. I was a couple of inches shorter, and had this dark beard, and Afro hair. We looked the part and so we tried to act the part.

I kept begging the police department to get me an undercover car to use. They kept telling me no. So I either borrowed a car from a friend or family member, rode with the crooks or CI, or parked the detective car down the street and walked to the deals.

Earlier in my undercover career I was involved in a burglary and fencing ring. One of the main characters in this gang was a used car salesman. He would buy just about anything, and he didn't care if it was recently stolen. I went with a snitch a couple of times while we offloaded hot items. The CI would tell the car dealer that the items had just been stolen from a home or business. I was introduced as one of the crooks who had broken into the places. After the third visit, I arranged for a visit to the car lot and the selling of what was labeled as stolen property from a residential burglary. My problem was transportation. I didn't have an undercover car and the department was too cheap to rent me something.

I went home and got my own pickup truck, loaded up the "stolen property", and drove to the car lot. I met with the dealer and completed the transaction, then I headed for the police department to write up the case and get search and arrest warrants. I was at the station for about a half hour when the desk sergeant came to tell me that I needed to call my house. I dropped what I was doing and called my wife at our home. She wanted to know who the hell the car dealer was who called the house and was asking her a thousand questions. She also wanted to know who was "Doc" and why was he driving my pickup. I explained what had happened and she calmed down. I never shared with her what I was doing at work, but thankfully she had enough sense to not answer any questions from the car dealer.

I called the car dealer and told him he had upset a family member when he called the house. I told him I had borrowed a brother in law's truck, and they did not know what I was involved in. I chewed his ass out royally and told him that now I didn't have any transportation. He said he had copied down the license plate number on the pickup and then looked it up on the State of Washington data base for vehicles. He said he wanted to get in touch with me to make more purchases.

I told my partners that I was done with that case, as I didn't need the crook finding out that a cop was selling him stolen items. He now knew where I lived. We waited a while then sent another UC in with the first informant and got the whole gig going again. The car dealer and his stolen property ring were soon arrested.

Being without a UC car was a real hindrance so I had no choice…I stole a car.

GRAND THEFT AUTO

Or as I liked to call it: "Misappropriation of City Property." Bob and I had been assigned an undercover detective car, a beige, four door, 1972 Dodge with red grill lights and a siren. A police radio was bolted to the transmission hump. I could drive anywhere and someone would immediately yell, "Cop!" How am I going to buy dope with this car? I can't even go and meet a CI without him becoming all paranoid. "I'm not getting in that car! Get away from me before everyone knows I'm hanging out with the police!"

The way things worked in the department was each team of narcs had a car assigned which was kept at the police station and used during your shift. I just changed the rule a little bit. I took our car home on a Friday after work, and by Monday had made a few changes. I had connections with wrecking yards and parts dealers throughout the county. I was always fixing up hotrods or classic cars. I picked up a set of mag wheels, and had them mounted on the car tires. I obtained a set of shackles and bolted them to the rear leaf springs which raised the back of the car into the air. I took the police radio out and threw it in the trunk, but hooked up an AM/FM radio to the police Motorola speaker. Lastly, I bought two cans of brown primer and sprayed wherever I thought it would look good. I sprayed the right front fender, part of the trunk, and around the wheel wells.

I called Bob on Monday and told him I would pick him up that evening. I got a surprised look when I pulled into his driveway.

"Here Bobby, have a beer and we'll christen our new Narc-mobile."

Each day or night when we went to work, I would park the car about two blocks away from the station. I didn't want any dope dealers seeing it around the station, and I sure as hell didn't want my sergeant to spot it. About a week after the transformation, Bob and I were driving around with a CI and heading to make a marijuana buy. We picked up the dealer in an apartment near 84th and Hosmer, and we hadn't gone a block when the crook says, "Damn! This looks just like a police car."

I responded, "Use to be. I bought it at an auction. Look. See the little switch on the dash, right next to the stick on label

that says “Lights and Siren.” They even left that on.”
From the back seat I heard, “Cool!”

A few months went by with Bobby and me driving the “borrowed” detective car when out of the blue one day the sergeant says, “Get all of your gear to include guns, badges, handcuffs, vests, radios, and ID cards. I have to do a yearly inventory. Oh! I also have to inspect your detective car, but I can’t find it.”
“Look sarge. The car is fine. You don’t really need to see it, do you?”
“Yes I do! Where is it?”

I told him it’s across the street hidden in an underground parking garage. We walked over and he just stood there with his mouth hanging open. “I’ll lose my sergeant stripes. They will can me. What have you two done this time?”
I explained that everything was just cosmetic and could be put back in a couple of hours. I even showed him how a little light rubbing compound would take the primer right off. He was finally convinced that he might not get fired, so he agreed to talk to the lieutenant and captain and see if we

could keep the car. They all agreed with the caveat that no one else had better find out.

Since I was into larceny a bit I expanded my horizons. Most cops will deny this fact, but they are a gullible bunch. I was sent to Fort Belvoir, Virginia by the Army Reserves to attend a two week training class. Present were going to be about three hundred Special Agents/Criminal Investigators from all over the world, and the subject matter was cop stuff.

At the end of the two weeks, I felt the need to treat myself to a glorious night out at the Fort Belvoir Officers Club. However, funds were short and payday was nowhere near. So I got all dressed up in my military uniform with the four rows of combat ribbons, topped with my aviator wings, and set-off by my prized Good Conduct Medal. I procured a clip board and a roster of all attendees. I then went from barracks to barracks and hit every room I could find with the plea for everyone to chip in $1.00 to purchase parting gifts for the instructors. I had guys giving me a dollar, and one for their room mate who was out somewhere. By the time I finished I had $250.00.

I hit the officers club running at 4:00 p.m and found myself a great table with a view of the Potomac River. After cocktails and appetizers, I settled down to a bottle of wine and then ordered the Surf and Turf, which had a nice lobster tail as the fish half.

I was on my third bite when who should walk in but four of my class mates, all reservists from my unit and members of the Seattle Police Department. They stood at my table and gave me the stink eye. *"Uh. Hi guys. I'm lonely as hell here with this big table all to myself. Why don't you get a menu and join me? I'm buying."* I figured if they were full and half-drunk, they would have some difficulty beating the shit out of me.

CAPERS WITH THE STATE NARCS

Washington State had started a Narcotics Unit patterned after the DEA. They were supposed to use their resources and personnel to assist police departments by providing undercover officers and money. The next thing I knew we had a guy named Paul, assigned to us, from the state. He looks like a biker except that he was about 5'5'' and 150 pounds. The state rented him an apartment in downtown Tacoma, and the only ones who knew about this arrangement were Bobby and me. We would introduce him around and use him to make drug buys.

The one big drawback to working as a narc in Tacoma at the time, was that you could never give out an address or phone number to the crooks. You just didn't have one to give. There were a lot of suspicious people we were dealing with and it never helped to always tell them, "No. You can't call me or come over. Give me your address and phone number and I'll call you." Now, with our new biker buddy and downtown apartment, we could really operate like legitimate dopers.

I got a call from Paul one day around the first of July '78, telling me he had made a connection with some bikers who were dealing speed. The crooks were supposed to bring thirty pounds of marijuana and 6,000 tablets of speed for the initial buy. It everything went well then additional weed and speed would be available. A deal was set-up to take place at the Tacoma Narrows Airport in a week. The bikers were told they were going to be selling to business men from Alaska. They would be flying in to take possession of the drugs and would bring the cash, which in this case was $100,000. Paul would be there to make the introductions, and two other state guys would be in the airplane playing the part of the business men. Up in the tower would be a state surveillance guy. Bobby and I would be hiding and help with the takedown and arrests. This was to be a simple buy/bust operation. The bikers would show the drugs. The state would show the money. Bobby and I would show the guns and badges.

A few days prior to all of this going down, I got a call from the Puyallup Police Department. They had a detective, Joe Sokolic who had gotten promoted and was now assigned to be their narcotics officer. The department wanted to know if

Joe could ride with Bobby and me for a week or so to learn the ropes.

"Send him on over. We'll try not to let him corrupt us."

Joe spent a few days riding with us and watching how we did dope buys and worked our informants. This was a cram course on doing hand-to-hand buys and the follow-up search warrants. Then we told him about our buy/bust scheduled for the airport and invited him along to watch how the big boys did things.

We arrived on the appointed afternoon at the Tacoma Narrows Airport and met with Paul. He showed us where all the parties would be meeting, and then we checked the time for the plane's arrival. The state guys and the plane with the money would arrive first. Then the bikers would make their appearance. This was to take place around 5 p.m. The airport covered 644 acres and had a lot of wooded areas surrounding it. There were also hangers and airplanes parked near the runway. The runway itself was about 5000 feet long and was generally north to south. There was a parking lot to the east of the tower. Between the parking lot and the airplane parking area was a large steel Conex container, which measured approximately eight feet by eight feet, and was twenty feet long. Conexs' were used for shipping freight on trains and boats. With all of these obstacles and hiding places what could possibly go wrong?

The plan called for Bob and me, armed with shotguns, to hide inside the container. The steel doors faced where the airplane would park, so we could see the signal to make the arrests. We would be blind to the delivery car which would park behind the Conex, and we would have to exit and converge on the car and arrest those occupants. Joe would be joining us in the Conex, but he was just there to be an observer.

At 4:30 p.m. we were all in place. The plane landed and the two state actors were standing near the wing dressed in flashy suits. Paul, who looked like a garage sale reject, was standing with them. Bobby, Joe and I were in the box with the doors partially opened. I was bored; really, really bored. I thought what was needed was a little levity and humor. I figured I should enlist poor Joe in on my scheme because Bobby wouldn't do it. As word came down from the tower surveillance agent that the biker's car was coming onto airport property, Paul and the other two state guys all turned toward the parking lot which put them in line of sight with the Conex. At that time, I told Joe to open the doors a little wider, and as soon as he did, I dropped my pants and mooned the state guys.

There was no time for them to yell at me or to take any kind of other action, like shoot me. All they could do was stand there looking expectantly at the bikers, who couldn't see me.

Two of the bikers walked past the Conex while we hid from view. As soon as he reached the airplane a conversation was started and one of them showed the UC a bag which contained some of the drugs. The UC checked the bag and then gave the signal for the take down. Bobby and I ran out the doors and each of us turned a different direction to head for the parking lot and arrest whoever was in the car. I heard a shot and didn't wait to find out who had popped one off. The car, a '77 Chevrolet Monte Carlo with Missouri plates, was now moving and heading right at Bob and me. I started pumping rounds into the car. I had four rounds of double ought buck in my gun. I shot the hood and hit the radiator and driver's side front tire. Bobby, also packing a shotgun, hit the front end and the engine area and windshield. The car fishtailed, spun around, and headed out of the parking lot. We both fired again at the rear end. When last seen the car was headed north at a high rate of speed and quickly disappeared. We had hidden our car behind a hanger and couldn't get to it, but we called for backup and put-out an APB on their car.

We walked back to join the others and at this time Joe said, "Holy shit! Did you guys see that? There was a guy in the back seat of the car sitting behind the driver, and he had a rifle. As soon as you guys came around the corner heading for the parking lot, he fired at you!"
Had I known that I wouldn't have been shooting just to stop the car?

Thinking quickly, Bob and I both said, "Yep! Saw the rifle and heard the shot before we opened up on that car."
I had been a little too hasty in previous confessions and didn't need more time off.

The two undercovers in the plane and Paul had the crooks under arrest. These dumb shit bikers had tried to rip off the cops and were packing pistols. Too much of their own product up their noses. They thought it would be an easy target. Just as we were getting the bust signal, they went for their guns to try a rip. The original buy was to be for 30 pounds of marijuana and 6,000 hits of speed with 300 more pounds of weed and 300,000 speed tabs if everything was good. The crooks thought that the out of town buyers were carrying the agreed upon $111,000.

Police and Sheriff units arrived and then fanned out to look for the car. They finally found it hidden in some bushes to the west of the airport. It had the hood and radiator shot up and two flat tires. It's a wonder it made it as far as it did. Inside the car the officers found marijuana and a rifle. A canvass of the neighborhood found a resident who had seen two guys with duffle bags hitchhiking. The state interrogated the two arrestees and eventually got warrants for the other two. Joe said he was going back to nice quiet Puyallup and he didn't really want to hang around with two crazy narcs from Tacoma.

There was a bar called "The Barbary Coast" near the intersection of Jefferson and Commerce streets. The bar was a notorious gay hangout, and we received reports that the bartender was dealing coke. Our sergeant told me to get Bob and Paul and go down there to make some buys. That night we walked into the Barbary at 8 p.m. and grabbed a table right near the front door. This was a small, round table pushed up against the wall facing the bar. I was seated on the left side with my back to the wall. Paul was sitting next to me with his back to the bar. Bobby was sitting on the right side also with his back to the wall. Bob had been in the Navy. He knew all about keeping your ass against something impenetrable.

We ordered drinks, and within a few minutes one of the patrons slid over and asked if we needed anything else. I told him we were interested in buying some coke, and he told me he could fix-me-up. He then walked over to the bar and started whispering in the bartender's ear. A short time later the bartender came over to our table and knelt down right in front of me.

"Hi. I understand you want to buy a little coke."
I told him, "Yes."

Then he said, "I can get you all you need" and with that he starts running his hands up and down my leg.

I was packing a snub nose 2 inch .38 in an ankle holster, and this guy was just moments from finding that out. I was also packing a six-incher in my pants and hoped the bartender wasn't looking for that. Paul grabbed the guy's arms and pulled him back, and told him, "He's with me. We are a couple."

He then placed both his hands on top of my knees to prove it and moved between me and the bartender. It was loud as hell in there and we had to shout in each other's ear to be heard. I leaned over to the bartender, pointed at Bob, and said, "He's available." The bartender says,"Yeah? I was looking at him, but he looks mean. He is so butch!"
I told the crook, "It's all an act. He is really gentle, and right now has no one to share moonlit walks with."

Meanwhile Bobby was yelling in my other ear: "What are you two talking about, and why does he keep blowing me kisses?"

I told Bob that everything is going great and we will make the buy soon. Bob started fidgeting, and then told Paul and me that he has to pee. I yelled back that the bathroom is down the hall, but Bob says he ain't going alone. A few minutes later, Bob says he is going out to the front doorway to buy some cigarettes out of the machine. As soon as he left, I got up and went down the long hallway to the men's room. I used the facilities and then headed back to our table.

As I was coming back up the hall, Bob came running toward me and yelled, "Come back in there with me." I told him no. He had to go so bad that he had no choice but to continue into the men's room. I took a few more steps and two guys holding hands passed me on the way to the bathroom. Bobby seemed so paranoid I thought perhaps I should return to the men's room and help allay his fears.

I turned and headed back the way I had come and followed them into the room. Bob heard them enter, but had his back to them. I came in, walked up behind Bob and grabbed him around the waist.
I snuggled up and said, "Hi big boy!"
Bobby levitated. I swear he left the ground and was hovering

three feet off the floor. I could have signed him up for helicopter flight training. I realized he was only getting up on his tiptoes to put as much distance as possible from whoever was trying to mate with him. From the nearby urinals could be heard giggling, and exclamations of, "Oh! Aren't they cute?" I let go and was laughing so hard I thought I would fall down. I didn't want to bend over with laughter. Not in that place. Bobby was trying to pee and giving me the evil eye at the same time. He was also looking at the other two patrons and thinking, "I can't kill Lazares - too many witnesses."

I ran back to the table, and got on my side as quickly as I could and sat down. Paul meanwhile had scored the coke, and we were ready to leave.

I was suspicious of Paul. He didn't weigh a buck fifty with his leathers on, and I suspected he may have some fetishes going on. He had no Harley, but did own several pairs of rawhide thongs.

He volunteered to return to the Barbary by himself and continue with the drug cases. Paul made a few more buys from the bartender on several occasion, and we eventually got a warrant and had him arrested. This took a couple of weeks, all of which were spent with Bob not talking to me.

PINKIES AND TIME OUTS

I was doing some deals with the Thurston County Sheriff and we were trading snitches back and forth. Bob and I had a pretty good CI who was in the Army at Ft. Lewis and he was buying drugs everywhere. This huge post shared a border with Pierce County and Thurston. Most of us detectives had joint commissions enabling us to work and make arrests in the city of Tacoma and Pierce County. We didn't have one with Thurston, so we had to call them when we had information on dealers, or were going to make a controlled buy using the CI.

Our CI was loaned-out to the Thurston County guys and they made some buys from a meth dealer who lived on a farm. When it came time to make the raid and affect the arrests of all involved, I got a call inviting us to go along.

Arrangements were made to meet in Olympia at a bar for some lubricant. You can't be doing door and ass kicking with a dry throat. The arrest team did a chalk-talk and mapped-out where we were going and who was getting arrested. The farm was located near Black Lake and we would not have the element of surprise. The crooks would be able to see us coming when we turned off the main road, so the plan was to go in fast. There were about a dozen of us cops and we would be in several cars. I was assigned to a crew and was told I would be riding out to the raid in a pickup truck with a camper on the back. A couple of other cops and I would be in the camper.

Needless to say, a few beers had been tipped while working out the game plan. I got into the camper and we started caravanning out of town. There was one lead car, my vehicle, and two more cars behind us. We stopped at a traffic light, and this dim plan began to emerge in my mind. By the time we hit the next light, the plan gained clarity, and at the third light, I sprang into action.

I threw open the rear door of the camper, turned around, dropped my pants, and mooned the cops in the two cars behind me. However, the light was a little shorter than I anticipated and the truck pulled out, dumping me in middle of the street. Both cars were honking at me as I tried to get upright and pull my pants up. This was late afternoon in

downtown Olympia, and I had a lot of spectators. I was skinned up, and the truck I'm supposed to be in has left me. The guys behind don't want to let me in their car, as I am still hanging out; front and rear. Finally the laughter calmed down and I was allowed to squeeze into the back seat. The raid went off without a hitch, and we arrested several people involved in the manufacturing and selling of meth.
I also gained insight and maturity and never did another inappropriate thing during my career.

There was a large narcotic officer's training session and meeting scheduled for Spokane, so I wheedled a trip for Bobby and me. I loaded up our Narcmobile with a cooler full of beer, and jury-rigged an eight track player so we would have tunes. I picked up Bob at his house and away we went. We made it as far as North Bend, which is about fifty miles as the crow flies or twenty four beers. We ran out of beer so a stop was made to replenish the cooler.

As we passed Ellensburg, the empty bottles were piling up. Bob who was riding shotgun decided to show me trick shooting. He threw a bottle out the window and fired his .38 at it. Then when it smashed alongside I-90, he claimed to have hit it. So I grabbed a bottle and threw it across the hood, fired my .38 and also " claimed a hit." Pretty soon we were out of ammo and beer bottles, but a new problem arose. We were both about ready to burst. We needed a rest stop, and we needed it quick. I turned on the lights and siren and ran the needle up to about 100 mph. We soon spotted a turn for a rest stop and slid into a parking spot in front of the bathrooms. We both bailed out and ran for the urinal, but in my haste I left the car running along with the lights and siren. We came out of the men's room to a crowd of tourists staring at our car. There was also a very large contingent of seagulls flocking all over. In our attempt to run from the car to the toilet, a big bag of potato chips took a spill. The gulls were squawking and shitting on everything, so we beat a hasty exit back to I-90.

We arrived in Spokane and found the Ridpath Hotel. This historic hotel had been originally built in the 1800's but caught fire twice and had to be rebuilt in the 1950s. A lot of famous people had stayed in the hotel, to include Elvis and maybe Michael Jackson. Now it was our turn, but I couldn't find a parking spot to save my life. Plus, we both had to pee again. I circled the building and ended up going the wrong way on a one way street. I also spotted a parking space but it was sort of on the sidewalk. Oh Well! We won't be long. Pee and check in. How long could that take? By the time we came back out there were several parking violations stuck under the windshield wipers.

"Hey! The car isn't registered to me. Let's just throw them in the glove box."

A parking space opened up and I put the car in between two others. The only difference was they were facing east and I was facing west.

Bob and I got our room key and headed upstairs. When we arrived, we found we had been assigned a small room with no view. This will not do! The management must not know who they have in residence. We got into the elevator with our luggage and went up to the bridal suite on the top floor. We found a maid in the hallway and convinced her by showing our badges that we were now staying in this glamorous, oversized room. She let us in and we started unpacking. About five minutes later, the door opened and there stood the hotel manager. He shook his head and pointed to the door. I tried to convince him to let us stay. Nope! We gathered our stuff and returned to our original room.

That night we decided to tour Spokane and get something to eat and drink. When we went to our car, we found more tickets attached to the wipers.

"Into the glove compartment with your brethren."

We didn't stay out too late because we had already had a full day, and the training conference started early.

The next morning we were sitting in the back of the conference room when the first speaker started his welcome. This was the Chief of Police of the Spokane Department. He concluded his remarks by saying, "If there is anything I can do to make your stay more pleasant, let me know. If you experienced any problems while visiting us, be sure and get in touch with me."

My hand shot up.

"Yes! You in the back what can I do for you?"

"Well sir. It seems that I have acquired a fist-full of these parking tickets for no apparent reason."

"See my assistant after the meeting, and I'll need your name and your chief's phone number."

That night we were invited to the Spokane Police Officers Guild club house. There would be food and drinks. Sign me up! We got out there and about a dozen of us were all together having fun. The only spoilsport was a local DEA agent. Nice guy all day while he was sober. Complete asshole at night while drunk. He kept throwing his weight around and generally being a jerk, and we finally figured a way to get rid of him. We made plans to sneak out of the club and go to a bar called the Pine Cone.

I was standing in the parking lot when a fellow narc came out of the club with his girlfriend. We had all been laughing and joking, so in direct violation of my new found life plan, I dropped my pants and mooned her. She screamed, and got into the passenger side of her boyfriend's car and locked the door. A good friend of mine from Bellevue PD was with us. He and I had shared many years flying together in the Army, and he was not house broken.

He yelled, "That's nothing. Watch this."

He ran behind the car. Jumped on the trunk, and sprinted up over the top of the car. He then jumped down on the hood, dropped his pants and pressed his bare ass against the windshield.

The poor girl inside is now hysterical and curled up on the floor. The boyfriend is crying and trying to get his gun out. We calmed him down and told him everything would be alright. All he had to do is tell the police department he works for, that some criminal found out who he was, and vandalized his car.

He said, “That won’t work. I just bought that car for my wife, and she is going to kill me.”

The rest of the night was pretty uneventful except for being in the Pine Cone and having the DEA agent show up. It seems that I took offense to something he said and knocked him out. We finished the seminar and returned to Tacoma. On Monday, Bob and I got called into the Chief’s Office. While standing at attention in front of his desk, he informed us that neither one of us would ever leave the city limits of Tacoma again as long as he was chief.

I tried to tell him I didn’t do anything, “It was that asshole Yerbury, chief.”

“That’s fine. Sign here. The pink copy is yours. Yerbury! Don’t you move! You can sign as soon as Lazares is done.”

DOPE AND DOPES

There is a community located along the shore of Puget Sound called Salmon Beach. The homes were all built on pilings over the water and face toward the Gig Harbor Peninsula. There are spectacular views of the Narrows Bridge. The only drawback is you have to hike straight down to get there and straight up to leave. This community dates back to the start of the 20th Century. The little village was originally fishing cabins. I had a grandfather who had lived there with his brother when they first came to the U.S. from Greece in the early 1900's. Later in the 30's it was a haven for rum runners, and in the 60's, counter-culture took up residence. Hippies, dope smokers, tie dyed fashionistas, and people who just wanted to drop out.

On a beautiful afternoon, when he should have been fishing, a Tacoma detective was floating by the eighty or so cabins and he began to notice that growing in a lot of windows was Cannabis Sativa. Now he could have continued fishing and let the dope growers alone, or he could go get help. Another detective soon joined him, and the two of them wrote down the numbers of every house with marijuana growing. That turned out to be about nine cabins. They then returned to the police station and got search warrants for every single cabin on the list.

Bobby and I were still undercover and wanted no part of the raid, but they were short-handed and we had to help out. The raid was low key because there were some influential people living at Salmon Beach. It would also be an easy take down because there was nowhere to escape to, unless you wanted to swim for it across Puget Sound. The raid was planned for the following day, and we had a total of thirty-four officers involved.

Everyone gathered at the top of the cliff above Salmon Beach, and we started down the two trails. Every team had several search warrants, and at the bottom we spread out and began serving them. Somehow the word got out about the raid, and a Tacoma News Tribune reporter and photographer showed up. They wanted to chronicle the raid, and they wanted to get pictures of any undercover officers who were involved. There was no way Bob and I could leave the small houses without being seen and photographed. Somc of our fellow detectives threatened the news people, but that got them nowhere.

I then came up with Plan B. Bobby and I got the other guys to find all the marijuana plants that were ready for harvest and bring them to the cabin we were hiding in. They cut down sixty-six plants that were ready to harvest and brought them to us. When they arrived, the two of us gathered the plants in large armloads, completely camouflaging ourselves. We then walked out the door and up the hill to the parking lot. All that the photographer got was a picture of two pairs of legs and two large bundles of dope.

Lt. Sessions, who was in charge, interviewed a lady who stated that the community had been tipped-off the day before. She claimed she received several phone calls from the "prosecutor's office" warning her of the search and arrests. She failed to reveal why after the preemptory alert from the "snitch" she ended up being arrested with eight pounds of weed. Must have been smoking the evidence in an attempt to get rid of it. We ended up with over one hundred plants, some mushrooms, and LSD. There was a lot of indication that plants had been removed or destroyed prior to us arriving for the search.

Seattle P.D. Narcotics called me up and asked if I could help them with a controlled-buy and follow-up arrests. They had an informant who could purchase brown tar heroin from some Mexicans. This was to go down in Tillicum, a small town out near Fort Lewis. The Seattle crew had no idea where anything was. Then I would also have to write up a search warrant and get it signed by a Pierce County Judge. The Seattle guys had no jurisdiction in our area.

Bob and I loaded up with the Seattle narcs and headed to Tillicum. We watched their CI go into a small house and then exit a short time later. He was met in a parking lot and gave his controllers a small balloon of suspected heroin. The Seattle team field tested the contents and confirmed it was heroin. I took one detective with me back to the police station while Bob and the rest of the crew watched the crook's house. I typed-up a search warrant and then called around and found a judge home. We went out and got the warrant signed and then raced back to Tillicum. Meanwhile, we had called the Pierce County Sherriff's Office to get some uniformed officers assigned. We were working in their jurisdiction and there was nothing worse than to have a bunch of cops trying to arrest you because someone had reported long haired derelicts with guns going into a house. That happened on more than one occasions in previous arrests when we were a little hasty in storming a house.

We kicked-down the doors and stormed in. The search resulted in us finding heroin, coke, cash and guns. The heroin was valued at over $250,000, and we got $9,000 in cash. We also arrested three Mexican nationals who were in the country illegally. Since Seattle had no jurisdiction, Bob and I got the arrests and evidence, but we also got all of the paperwork.

A week went by and I got called by the Seattle guys. They said they needed a copy of the paperwork and would gladly drive down to pick it up. They also said a party was in order. I went into our safe and found $50 in discretionary funds. I felt it was my discretion to spend it on drinks for the crew. We met the four guys from Seattle at a local bar, and I laid the $50 on the table and said we would drink until the fifty was gone. The sergeant-in-charge of the visiting narcs reached into his shirt pocket and pulled out two $100 bills, and said, "No, our treat and we'll drink until this is gone."

There was a band playing and the S.P.D. gang started dancing with some girls from the bar. Then they started yelling for the band to play the stroll. A couple of these cops were older than the rest of us. As a matter of fact, there was some dirt on the floor and they were also older than that. The band did a rendition of the stroll, and the two cops started yelling that they next wanted to hear a limbo tune. I got up and went and found the kitchen, stole their broom and returned. Bobby and I held the broom while this guy did the limbo.

One drink led to another and pretty soon the coats came off. There were six of us crammed into a booth all packing guns on our hips or in shoulder harnesses. The customers, who had been dissenting to our music choices, now became absent patrons. Pretty quickly the bar was empty except for the band, us narcs, and the girls the S.P.D. guys were dancing with. The poor band was required to play the limbo, followed by the stroll, followed by the limbo, ad nauseam. The band also seemed reluctant to take a break; I think they really liked us. We finally "closed the bar," called it a night, and headed for our respective homes.

It was an entirely different breed of cop who chose to work narcotics. I think that you had to be borderline whacko and some of the things I experienced would only add credence to that theory.

I went to a narcotics conference in Vancouver on my own time. The chief sure wasn't going to let me go anywhere. We all stayed at the Red Lion located right on the Columbia River. The entire trip was a replay of Spokane, except a narc from a small central Washington town, got into a fight with his girlfriend. Rather than just punch her out, or better yet punch himself out, he walked out the door at the front of the hotel lobby and shot himself in the head. Talk about your wet blanket party-pooper.

A few months later I attended another soiree at the Longview Red Lion. Again, I went on my own time, but I got the U.S Army to pick up the tab. This was a lot tamer and more of an adult themed conference right up to the point where several narcs squared-off in the hallway to see who the better shot was. They paced it off to fifty feet and then began taking turns to see who could shoot out the light at the end of the hall. Management, not to mention the people in the guest rooms nearby, all took offense. The local P.D responded and threatened to lock everyone up, but then discovered a couple of their members had also participated.

Finding the Northwest contingent of law enforcement officers lacking in the sophistication that I had come to expect, I branched-out and sought the camaraderie of police officers from other jurisdictions. I found that not only the yokels from Washington State had conferences, but the entire state of California was hosting parties. I signed up and by using some influence with the U.S. Government, I was able to book myself on a trip to La La Land.

I obtained an all expense paid trip to Los Angeles for the purpose of going to school for two weeks on "Uncle Sugar's" dime. This was a class on "Dignitary Protection." While I did make an effort to attend classes, it was far easier not to attend classes. No one knew who I was nor did anyone care. The California guys had to get their tickets punched by attending and passing the courses, but I didn't.

I soon found myself hooked up with a Captain Dave from the L.A. County Sheriff's Office. He took me under his wing and vowed to show me a good time while I was in L.A. One Friday in class, he said since we had the weekend off; he had some fun scheduled. At three in the afternoon, I met him and we drove to the LAPD helipad. We met with the helicopter crew and then spent the next two hours flying all over greater L.A. in the police copter. They knew I had been a pilot in the Army, so they took great pains to make it a great flight.

We visited Watts, Hollywood, the Rose Bowl and Beverly Hills. When we landed at about 6:30 p.m, I was informed we were just starting the night. We drove down to the China Town district, and Dave steered me to a restaurant he knew. We entered and passed through the bar, where Dave snagged an old partner who was now an LAPD vice cop. This bar was like a scene from a Wambaugh book. There were a couple of off-duty cops in uniform drunk, and some hookers. Also present were a few groupies and the crazy vice guy. All we needed was a fat Chinaman; who then showed up at our table. 'Lim' owned the place and was friends with Dave from way back. Food started appearing, and there was no end to the entrees. One course would show up followed by another, and all the food was delicious. The owner sat with us and began telling stories about his travels. Lim informed us he was taking a group for a tour of Hong Kong, and that they were leaving next month. I told him that I had been in the Far East, but had never seen any part of China.

He looked over at me and said, “Do you want to go?”

I said, “That sounds interesting but I could never afford a trip like that.”

He then told me that it would cost me nothing.

I said something along the lines of, “How could I not have to pay?”

He turns to Dave who is rolling on the floor, laughing.

Lim looks at Dave and says, “You didn’t tell him about me, did you?

Dave replied, “Lim is as queer as a three dollar bill. If you go, you have to sleep with him.”

Lim stated, “Hong Kong has my favorite foods. My favorite dish is Lyk Sum Diq and Ah So Sum Yung Boi.”

I said, “I’m off Chinese food until further notice.”

I would hazard a guess that we ate and drank our way through about $300 worth of stuff. No bill showed up.

The whacked out vice cop said he was living on a boat in Marina del Rey and why don't Dave and I come down the following day for a boat ride.

Dave said, "Sure. Give me the directions and slip number."

I'm thinking: "Woo Woo! I'm going to ride around the marina and look at the movie stars' boats, in my own mini yacht."

The next morning, Dave picked me up and we drove out to Marina Del Rey. After we parked, we started looking for the correct pier and then proceeded down the dock looking for the correct slip. After a short walk, we found the boat which was just this side of being the dingy that takes you to the tender that will take you to the yacht. It was twenty-four feet of dry rot. The vice cop was living on this boat because wife number three had thrown his ass out of the house. There was a single bunk, a porta potty, and a hot plate. Everything this guy owned was lying on the deck, and nothing smelled very clean. He welcomed us aboard and started the engines. We cast-off the lines, and he reached down and grabbed two bottles of vodka. He handed one to Dave and he kept the other for himself. He then steered with one hand so as not to drop the vodka, which was clenched in the other hand. Dave and I are standing on the stern passing the vodka back and forth while whacko drove the “S.S Leaky” and pointed at real boats.

“That’s the one Natalie Wood was pushed off and killed.”

“That one belongs to John Wayne.”

“I believe somewhere below us is the Titanic.”

Blah-blah-blah!

The next thing Dave and I knew is that our skipper is shit-faced and has turned the corner and is heading around the jetty making for open seas.

“Hey guys. Do you want to visit Santa Catalina? It’s only twenty-three miles across the sea.”

“Dave. Do something. Shoot him! I can drive a boat.”

The theme song from Gilligan’s island kept going through my head. Dave convinced him we were done for the day and we headed back to the slip. Docking was just a little more difficult than our departure was, but we finally secured the boat and bid a fond farewell.

A few months later, I wrangled a trip to San Luis Obispo for another two week school with some of California’s finest. Again it was on Uncle Sam’s nickel, so TPD didn’t mind me taking the time off. The school was pretty uneventful, except for the night some of the guys thought it would be hilarious to put snakes in the instructor's bed. You wouldn't think that a few shots fired would generate that much response from the local police department.

"It's all fun and games until someone loses an eye."

One of the guys in my group was from Santa Barbara and he was regaling us with tales about Reagan's Ranch, which was in the hills above the coastline. He said he had a female deputy assigned to coordinate with the Marine contingent guarding the compound. The Marines were living in a motor home and trading shifts every twelve hours. The only problem that surfaced was that the deputy couldn't keep her gun belt on and her pants up. She was banging the gyrenes like a cheap screen door, and they weren't paying attention to their jobs.

"Winnebago Wendy." Keeping Marines happy since 1978.

I rented a car. Not just any car, but a Ford Pinto station wagon from "Rent a Dent." I needed transportation, but there was no money in the budget for a nice car. This heap had one window that wouldn't go up or down. It was just kind of in the middle. It also had a radio, but no antenna. I found a wire coat hanger in my room and straightened it out and then forced it down the hole in the fender where the antenna used to be. If I held my tongue just right, I could get one AM. station. One afternoon, another "convert to the light of redemption" and I, decided we needed to broaden our horizons. There was a country club located on the hills above the Pacific Ocean, and they had a bar. We decided we needed to mingle with the rich and famous, and give them a chance to view life at our level. As I pulled into the long driveway leading to the lobby of the club, there was nothing but Bentleys and Rolls. Each one was attended by a uniformed driver who was either polishing the car or standing there reading a newspaper. It looked like a scene out of "Chinatown." I pulled my Pinto to the curb in front of the reception desk and we both stepped out. The maitre d' came running out and could not contain himself. All I heard was: "Wha! Wha! Wha!"

He could not get any words to come out.

I said, "Hi! Got a bar?"

He pointed. We walked in and found this magnificent bar and grill overlooking the back nine of the golf course, and on the horizon, the Pacific Ocean. The manager followed us in and politely told us that if we just had one drink and left, he would be more than happy to pick up the tab.

"I'll have a double Wild Turkey on the rocks, and maybe one in a to-go cup. My new best friend over there is buying."

Graduation came, and we ended up booking a private room in F. McLintock's Saloon and Dining House, which was just off highway 101 across from the ocean at Pismo Beach. This was supposed to be a genteel affair attended by the representatives of law enforcement. What it ended up being was a drunken gathering of a bunch of depraved gun slingers. I knew we were in for a hell of a night when we sat down. The waiters arrived with the house specialty which was deep fried onion rings with homemade hot salsa. It took all of about three seconds for some cop from somewhere to challenge another cop to a chug-a-lug contest involving the hot sauce. The salsa came in twelve-ounce mason jars. A teaspoon of this shit would defrost a refrigerator. These fools were downing the whole jar to see who had the biggest cojones. Of course, they were drinking copious amounts of booze to cool the fire. Finally the food arrived and we began to eat our really good steaks.

"When all of sudden there arose such a clash, that we ran to our cars and tried to hide our stash."

Oops! Wrong poem. What really happened was a loud scream from the front entry way, followed by more screams from the hostess. We raced out to the entrance area because we figured one of us was being molested by a citizen. What we found was a lieutenant from Beverly Hills PD having sex with the restaurant mascot. Sort of! McLintock's had a real stuffed buffalo in the front entry way. The drunken lieutenant was standing behind the bison with his pants down around his ankles, pretending to have sex. Or maybe not! You never knew with those California fruits and nuts. Again a kind management agreed to pick-up our bar tab if only we would go someplace else to have dessert.

PAPER LIONS AND TOY TIGERS

Bobby was a pansy ass when I first teamed up with him. His idea of a cocktail was to order a Tom Collins. He admitted that what he really liked was the cherry, and the finer establishments put a little umbrella in his drink. It wasn't long before I introduced him to Scotch, and thus began his downfall.

One Christmas we were working and decided we should attend as many parties as we could get ourselves to. This also meant we would be drinking on duty while driving a stolen police car.

"I can't break the law, I am the law."

It says so right on the commission card the chief gave me.

It wasn't long into the Christmas Eve pursuit of Santa when Bob mentioned he was seeing elves, or maybe midgets dressed as elves. I always took Bobby at his word ever since the time he may or may not have seen the UFO, or what he thought might be a UFO. I never could get a straight answer from him about that night. I do know that an anal probe will addle the brain.

We were making the rounds of our Christmas cohorts and friends, and found our way to an auto body shop on Pacific Ave. By that time we may have had a couple of cocktails, but that only made it easier for the next few to slide on down. I parked Bob in a chair by the roll up doors and went in search of something to eat. A few minutes later I walked over to Bobby, and he's holding a large, round tray which may have been a hubcap from a Lincoln. He looked up at me and said, "You should try this granola. It's really good."

The owner of the shop came over and grabbed the tray from Bob and told him, "You dumb shit! You're eating the floor sweep I put out for ashtrays!"

It's easy to mistake kitty litter for a snack with too much Christmas cheer.

One night Bob and I ended up in a South Tacoma bar looking to see if anyone was selling dope. There was a little alcove away from the bar and patrons, where we could stand and observe what was going on inside the place. Nothing much seemed to be happening, so we decided to have just one drink. I ordered my usual and Bobby said, "Hey! This lady says I should try a drink called a Toy Tiger!"

"What the hell is that?" I asked.

"I don't know. It has a bunch of stuff in it and Chartreuse Liquor. It can't be too bad. She says they are really mild and she drinks them all the time. Maybe they will put a cherry and umbrella in it for me."

This green drink showed up and I got offered a taste. I couldn't get past the smell, which was something akin to turpentine and aftershave. Bob started slurping them down. He had about three of them, and told me they are a sissy drink and he can't even feel them yet. A minute later he disappeared. I mean poof! I thought maybe the Lord had come and taken him away. He was gone. A few minutes later, the lady who introduced him to this drink came around the corner and said to me, "I think you need to check on your partner. He is lying on the floor in the ladies' restroom and I don't think he's breathing."

I went into the bathroom and there was Bob. He was semi-conscious and had managed to throw-up all over his shoes.

I didn't want to touch him, let alone pick him up off the floor. But if I left him there, someone would call the cops.

Bobby and I were out buying drugs a few days later and were doing our deals out of a van we procured from the impound lot. We were parked in front of a house near 62nd and Pine and were planning on doing a buy/bust. Sgt. Madera and our backup were hiding nearby, and would provide security and help with the arrests. A lady came out of the house and joined us in the van. She pulled a pound of marijuana from under her clothes for us to buy. I grabbed the woman and placed her under arrest. Bobby headed to the house thinking everyone was following him. He was leading the charge to get in and arrest the main man. He kicked in the door and entered yelling, "Police!"

He turned around and no one had followed him into the house. He was now all alone with a bunch of crooks looking at him. He did the only sensible thing and started screaming, "You are all under arrest! Don't anyone move!"

By now the place was filled-up with cops and they spread throughout the house rounding people up. All of a sudden there were sounds of gunfire. One of the backup detectives had confronted the home owner who pointed a rifle at him. The officer shot and wounded the armed suspect, then cuffed him on the floor. Medics were requested along with Robbery/Homicide detectives to do an "Officer Involved Shooting Investigation."

A few weeks later the wounded suspect hung himself from an apple tree in his front yard. After he bailed out of jail, I guess he just didn't want to spend time in prison.

Bobby and I were driving around looking for some dope to buy, or at least hoping to find a doper with some narcotics in his pocket. The drug dealers had refined their methods of carrying contraband by sticking it in balloons, and then putting all of this in their mouth. They thought wrongly that they could swallow the balloons and avoid arrest.

This brought up two unique methods for recovery of the illicit drugs. The first scenario required arresting the dealer and then putting him in a cell with no toilet. It was then a matter of waiting for the balloons to pass. Or more humanely, the dealer would be taken to the hospital and given a laxative by the E.R. doctor. Then they were handcuffed to a bed and the waiting game would begin.

"Ooh! Your face is all scrunched up! Are you in a little distress? Oh Look! Balloons. It must be your birthday."

The evidence was then collected and saved for the trial after the "Doc Eagleston Test."

"Yup! Tastes like shit."

"No Doc. Check the contents inside the balloon."

The second method was not humane at all, but a lot more fun. We would hide and watch a dealer until we were certain he was holding his dope in his mouth. We would then sneak up on the crook and wait until the last possible moment to surprise him. He would start swallowing the minute he saw or heard us. We in turn would jump on him. One of us would go high and the other would go low. If I was the high man, I would firmly place both hands around the neck of the suspect so as not to allow him to swallow. This also caused some thrashing about on the dealer's side of the equation because this also cut off all air to his lungs. Some times we were treated to a version of the "Funky Chicken." While I am helping the asshole to find Jesus, Bobby would start placing his fist firmly in the stomach area of the dealer. If the dealer had swallowed any contraband, it would start making its way back to his mouth where it could be recovered by us. This technique was later refined by the medical profession and called "The Heimlich Maneuver." I invented this evidence recovery method after I got a life saving award. My wife and I were having lunch in the basement of the Bon Marche at the Tacoma Mall. A fat lady was sitting at the counter when she started choking. I jumped up to do the Heimlich and couldn't get my arms around her to do the maneuver. So I kept slamming her stomach into the counter top until she blew the obstruction out.

STREET CRIMES

Someone finally figured out that Bobby and I were having way too much fun working in narcotics. We were asked if we wanted to join a new unit being formed up by Lt. Bud White. So, in October of 1979, we reported to the Street Crime Unit.

Bobby and I departed narcotics with a "TPD Exemplary and Meritorious Service Award."
It read in part that we were given extreme latitude in the investigation of narcotic trafficking: **"With only one rule, to keep their immediate supervisor informed as to their actions."**

Oh Hell yes! *"Sit down sarge and let us tell you what we have been doing."*
Every time we tried that approach our sergeant would place his hands over his ears and then respond with the same words, "I don't want to know. If I know, then I can be held responsible. Go away!"

"As a result of their work, Yerbury and Lazares were responsible for the arrest of 23 persons for unlawful possession of controlled substances, 11

others for unlawful delivery of a controlled substance, and 3 others for miscellaneous felonies."

It would have been even bigger arrest numbers, but a lot of the apprehensions were made by other detectives to keep our name and face out of the reports.

The new unit was called Street Crimes, and there would be four of us assigned. Besides Bob and me, Bruce Jackson and Bill Garrison would be working in the unit. Our missions were to respond to areas where a lot of crime was taking place, and then nip it in the ass. There might be a bunch of purse snatches taking place in one section of town, or strong arm robberies in another. Sometimes armed robbers would pick an area of the city or a certain type of business, and then we would start doing surveillance on those stores or gas stations in the hopes of catching the bad guys. Wherever a crime pattern showed-up, we would get the assignment and try to make an arrest.

"Every Friday night between 10 p.m. and midnight, two idiots wearing President Nixon face masks are robbing one of the 7/11 Stores in the south end of Tacoma. See if you can arrest them, or at least make them switch to Kennedy masks. I'm a Republican."

One of our first tests was a spree of perverts wagging their willies in the men's room in Wright Park at night. Wright Park was twenty-seven acres of lawn and over 300 trees. It was bordered on the north by Division Street, and 6th Ave on the south. It sat between I street and G Street. The crook or crooks were getting bolder, and it was only a matter of time before someone was going to get hurt. Bobby and I got the assignment and worked out our strategy. I drew a diagram of the park and sketched in all the flora and fauna. I added the paths and walkways, and the fountains and ponds. I showed all the points of ingress and egress. Or at least that is what should have been done. What we had was a plan that consisted of us wearing old clothes and climbing a tree. From that vantage point, we could drop down on the weenie waver and end his criminal career.

Bobby and I used to spend many a night in Wright Park when we were on patrol. One of us would get out on one side and the other would go to the opposite end of the park. We would then walk toward each other to see what we could scare out of the bushes.

"Oh Officer! I am so glad you come along! Some mean man tied me to this tree and pulled my pants down. Now I seem to have slivers in my woodie."

We waited for darkness and crept into the park. We found the main path in the middle of the park and then climbed up into an elm tree. We were not up there for more than a half hour when two males came sauntering down the trail holding hands.

"Pssst! Bobby, maybe they know something, let's jump down and ask them."

With that we leapt to the ground right behind the two and said, "Hi guys!"

There was a mighty scream and the two of them took off for parts unknown yelling, "Help! Police! Help!"

We looked at each other and telepathically knew that we just might be causing a heart attack. We figured we should chase these guys and explain that we are the cops. Now there are four people running through Wright Park. Two are yelling, "Help! Police!" And two are yelling, "Stop you dumb assholes! We are the police!" They looked back and all they can see is two guys with long hair, and old clothes chasing them. We never got within a block of those two, and for all I know, they are still running.

Lt. White came into our little office and told us that there had been a lot of reports of strong arm robberies on Commerce Street between 13th and 15th. "Put an end to it and put someone in jail."
"OK Boss!"

I went down to the property room and rummaged around until I found a pair of bib overalls and a ratty shirt. Bobby and I then went to the liquor store, and I bought a cheap pint bottle of bourbon. After dressing in my new uniform, I splashed some booze on myself, took a healthy snort for good luck, and then put the bottle in my back pocket. Bob dropped me off a block away, and I walked down to a vacant doorway next to Ezzie's Attic near the corner of 13th and Commerce. Ezzie's was a thriving bar and attracted a lot of low-life's. The plan was for me to lay in the doorway until I was robbed by someone. Then Bobby and my backup would swoop down and arrest the bad guy. I did my part and wasn't lying there for more than ten minutes when this guy starts nudging me. I was playing like I was unconscious and he is pretending he is concerned about my health.
"Hey man, are you okay? Let me take your watch off so I can check your pulse with the second hand."

Then he started to tug on my wedding ring. I forgot I was wearing it and I didn't want to lose it so I grumbled, and then pulled both arms under my body. I lay there for another minute or so, and then the crook started going through my pockets. I had a wallet stuffed in a back pocket with a few dollars in it and this is what he went for. As soon as he had the cash he started to leave and I gave the signal for the arrest. And then I gave the signal for the arrest. And then…

No one was rushing to my rescue and going after the bad guy. I stood up and started yelling, and everyone finally showed up and the chase was on. They had been busy regaling each other with stories of daring do and forgot about watching me.

Bob and I ran after the crook who ducked into a porn shop. We came steam rolling right behind him and tackled him among the racks of books and movies. He got punched a few times and then turned over and handcuffed. The store clerk is screaming and yelling for the cops, and again we are yelling, "We are the cops." I'll bet we did a few hundred dollars worth of damage to the store and its contents. The guy we arrested was named Henry P, and several years later

Bobby was entering a restaurant when he ran into Henry. Henry did a double take and then asked if Bob was one of the guys who arrested him downtown, and destroyed the porno place.

Bob said, "Yes" and Henry laughed and replied, "You guys scared the shit out of me. I'm a "strong armed robber", but I thought I was getting mugged."

We figured that this had all worked out pretty well and I was eager to try being the decoy again. A few nights later we set up on Commerce, only this time we were near 15th and I was lying on the sidewalk across the street from the businesses. It didn't take long and I was getting rolled again. This time I got punched a little after the asshole took my wallet, but lesson learned. Bobby was watching and was hot on his trail. I jumped up and joined in the chase across Commerce. We caught up with our guy right in front of a store front Gypsy joint.

The Gypsies were always running scams from these places, such as fortune telling or tarot card reading. Or the young Gypsy girls would sit in the windows showing as much skin as they could. A guy would walk by and think maybe the girl was a prostitute. He would go in and start to get friendly, and then the girl's father and brothers would show up and throw the guy out. Once outside, he would discover his wallet was missing. When he tried to get back inside, he would find the door locked and all the lights off. I investigated an assault crime one time related to the Gypsies. The victim thought he was buying time with a hooker and gave her some money which she immediately shoved down her blouse. When things didn't work out, he went after his cash. He said he stuck his hand down the front of her shirt and he instantly felt pain. He pulled his hand out and his thumb was gone. She had whacked it off with a straight razor so quickly, he hadn't even started to bleed. He then got thrown out the door by the family.

Another enterprise the Gypsies were into was selling cars. They would travel to Oregon and California and pick up a car, then resell it in Tacoma. The cars were cheaper in the southern states and there was no sales tax. There were a few guys in TPD who were always driving a fairly new car and there was a certain captain who always sported dealer plates. The plates belonged to the Gypsy, and this captain was always test driving a new car. Sometimes, he would test drive for six months. This was the same captain that I figured ratted me out to the dope dealer who ran the car lot.

Bobby and I caught up with the strong arm robber as he raced around a brand new Thunderbird sitting at the curb. A Gypsy was selling the car to a guy, and they were standing on the sidewalk talking business. Bobby and I ran right over the trunk and the roof of the car and tackled the robber. We then threw him on top of the hood and maybe bounced his head off the paint job a time or two. Then we introduced him to the latest dance craze, "The Funky Chicken."

You placed your hands firmly around the neck of your dance partner (crook) and then squeezed. When your partner got to the point where he was semi-conscious, you let loose of his neck. Your partner would then twist, jerk and spasm in his own version of the "Funky Chicken."

"I give the music a five, Dick. The dance moves get a ten though."

We got him handcuffed and face down on the sidewalk. The Gypsy was so hysterical he couldn't talk. He could only point at all the damage the two of us had done to his new car. The car buyer wanted no part of whatever was taking place and had sprinted down the street. We departed with our crook. The “Dynamic Duo” had struck again, and we basked in our glory. That was until the Gypsy called the department to demand an apology and cash for what we did to his car. I could just smell the “Pinky.” I was hoping that the damages wouldn’t come out of my pay check.

It had just turned to 1980 and crime was rampant. Bud White did a lot of analyzing of crime patterns, and was very good at what he did. He came in one afternoon and told us that there had been a rash of burglaries of dead people. In looking at the crime patterns it appeared that the burglars were reading the Tacoma News Tribune looking at obituaries. When someone old died, and had no immediate family nearby, the crooks would target the house while it was empty. They were cleaning the places out of antiques and jewelry. White told us that a recent obituary caught his eye and he thought we should set up on the house to see if the burglars showed.

Bud obtained a key to the house at 2316 North Alder and Bobby and I headed out as soon as it started to get dark. This was an old two-story home in the north end that had been built in the 1930s. We sneaked up on the place and let ourselves in through the front door. We then settled down on the living room floor with nothing but a police radio for company. As soon as it got dark, the house phone started ringing. Whoever was calling let it ring for some time and then waited a half hour or so and called back. This went on for a couple of hours.

About 9:30 p.m we could hear men's' voices outside and saw shadows moving around the house. Then we heard people at the front door knocking. They knocked loudly a few times and then left. A few minutes later they returned and knocked again. Only this time the knocking was followed by the front door being kicked in. Bobby and I were up and hiding against the living room walls when three men came hurrying into the house. We jumped out and yelled something sophisticated like, "Freeze you assholes! Police!"

They spun around and the chase was on. The burglars all sprinted out the door with us hot on their heels. As we chased them, we split into two groups and I had a couple of these guys in front of me, and they were possibly getting away. I did the only sensible thing I could think of. I fired a

warning shot into the air. Immediately one of them stopped dead in their tracks and I arrested him at gun point. As I was doing this I heard a second shot from a short distance away, and the words, "Stop! Or I'll shoot you!"
Bob showed up a minute later with another burglar in custody.

Now I started hearing sirens. When we first heard the knocking on the door, we requested back up, and when the door was kicked, in we yelled for help on the police radio. Now all of the police cars began arriving because some citizen has also phoned-in and reported there were shots fired. We met back in front of the victim's house and Bob and I each had a crook in custody. Sergeant Parkhurst walked up to us and was standing there with his pipe in his mouth. As we are telling our story the pipe took on a life of its own and started moving from one side of his mouth to the other. Right side. Left side. Back and forth the pipe went. Parkhurst finally asked, "There was a report of gunfire. Who got shot?"
I said, "Well sarge, I was in hot pursuit and they were getting away, so I fired a warning shot."

Now the pipe was moving at a really rapid pace back and forth, right- left- right- left, and Parkhurst says, "We don't fire warning shots!"

The pipe had become a blur, right-left-right-left, when Parky looked at us and said, "There was a report of more than one shot being fired."
Bobby jumped in front of me and looked right at Parky and told him with a straight face, "I fell down when I was chasing the bad guys and my gun went off accidentally."
I was choking and thinking about how in the hell I was going to get out from under this bus, where I had just been thrown by my faithful companion "Tonto."

We booked our two crooks and then started doing an investigation. It didn't take us long to figure-out who else was involved. We eventually got arrest warrants and search warrants, and ended up with all five burglars. We recovered a lot of the stolen property, and cleared up a bunch of crime. This band of crooks had been hitting places all over Pierce and King Counties.

Bobby and I received another award for "Exemplary and Meritorious Crime Fighting", and I got called into the chief's office to add another "Pinky" to my collection.
"We don't fire warning shots Lazares! Sign here."
"What about that asshole Yerbury, chief?"
"He will be attending a class on how to do foot pursuit, without tripping and hurting himself."

The next grand caper we were involved in was a sting operation. We joined forces with a couple of detectives from the Pierce County Sheriff's Office. Resources and talent were combined, and we opened a store front pawn shop on 6th Ave between Steele Street and Fife Street. We reached out to all of our snitches that they should spread the word among their brother crooks. They were to tell everyone that there was a pawn shop opened that would take stolen property, no questions asked.

It wasn't too long before we were doing a brisk daily business with burglars and dopers. They were constantly ripping people and houses off and now had a convenient place to unload their booty. A camera was set up to take pictures through a one way mirror. We simply took pictures of everyone who came in so we could match them with the stolen goods.

"Sure Mr. Smith. I'll buy your engraved silver place settings. Just what do the letters T.L on the forks stand for?"

"Tonsil Litus. It be my maiden name."

"Fine! Just step over to the mirror, smile and fix your Fro. I'll get your cash."

Since most of our clientele were dopers we also started buying drugs from them. Later, we got arrest warrants for everyone, and attempted to match the property with burglary cases.

HOMICIDE

Due to our stellar investigative techniques or again because they thought Bobby and I were having way too much fun, we were transferred to Robbery/Homicide. This was always the place where the elite of the elite detectives ended up. Somehow the police hierarchy made a mistake, and we were sent to the unit anyway. I occasionally thought that maybe we had just run out of units we could be transferred to.

"Hi chief. I have a vacancy in my unit. Who do you have available? Oh God! Not Lazares and Yerbury! They refuse to be supervised and are just a tad unorthodox! I would really like to make it to retirement and get my pension!"

We showed up the first of January 1982 and were given desks. There were two detectives to an office and our windows overlooked Tacoma Ave. The unit consisted of detectives assigned to sex crimes, armed robbery, major assaults and homicides. The sex guys pretty much just handled sex crimes and the rest of us handled everything else.

I worked Monday through Friday from 8 am to 4 pm like everyone else. In reality I worked a lot of overtime. Each morning we were given cases to work that came in during the night. Crimes that went down between 4 p.m and 8 a.m and were of significant import such as a major assault, a suspicious death or a homicide, meant one or more of us would be called-out from home to investigate the crime. Based on case load, one of the detectives would be assigned as the lead investigator and carry the case to its conclusion. Rarely a week went by that I didn't get a call at 2 a.m on a Friday or Saturday because someone was dead or thinking about being dead.

I hadn't been in the unit a week and Lieutenant Gilmore called me into his office and said, "There is a 'weenie waver' who has been showing up at the Tacoma Mall, and is harassing the girls who work at the Bon Marche. The employees have to park way out in a back lot and walk to the store. He drives up next to them while they are walking. He is completely naked and has been seen "spanking his monkey." Go figure a way to find him and arrest him."

I left the TPD offices and drove directly to the mall. I had a vested interest because my wife was working at Bon Marche. Whacking off I didn't care about, but I really didn't want her seeing and comparing 'simian sizes'. From the station to the mall was a twenty minute drive, and as I pulled into the northwest parking area, I spotted a car with a white male driving, and following a young lady toward the Bon. I pulled up behind him, hit my lights and siren, and pulled him over. I walked up to the driver's side window, and there sat, "Buck Naked" with a real stupid expression on his face. "Hi. I'm a cop and you and your primate are under arrest."

I cuffed him and threw him into the back seat of my car. I didn't know where his clothes were and could have cared less. If he liked riding around catching a draft, then that's how he was getting booked. I then got on the radio and requested dispatch to contact Gilmore. He soon answered on the radio and I informed him, "The famous weenie whacker is under arrest, and I hope I didn't take too long. I expected this case to take an hour, but it only took me thirty minutes." My reputation had been made: "David 17. Detective Smartass."

There were a lot of routine murders. Not exactly "Whodunits?" They were more on the order of, "She done it and the asshole had it coming." He shot her. She shot him. Family fights gone bad. But there were some real head scratchers too!

On August 6th, I got dispatched to a family fight with shots fired up on the Hilltop. The house was located just south of 23rd and K Street on the west side of the block. A smallish man named Nelson Sellers beat his larger wife, Pamela, and then shot her. He was seen loading her into the trunk of his car and driving off. Every local police department and the state patrol were notified to be on the lookout for the car and the suspect.

"Be on the lookout for a killer with a hernia. He's 5'5", 135 pounds and may now be wearing a back brace."

Our suspect turned himself into police officers shortly after the crime, but refused to reveal the location of the vehicle or the body.

I was informed the next day that the Pierce County Sheriff's Office had found the car in Lakewood. It was abandoned and there was no sign of the victim. The car appeared to have hit something in the road which caused the oil pan to rupture. The engine then must have seized up. Based on the location where the car was found, I did a circle from that point outward, which the car may have driven after losing all of its oil. Inside that circle was a large tract of uninhabited woods that bordered Ft. Lewis. Everything else was densely populated, and I didn't figure he would have dumped the body there. The PCSO provided their Search and Rescue vehicle, which was a motor home. We set up near the south end of McChord AFB in a field adjacent to Perimeter Road. To the south was the vast expanse of Ft. Lewis. There were numerous tank trails and goat paths running throughout the area, and I figured that our suspect had hit a rock either before or after dumping the body of his wife. All this was based on speculation, but I had to start somewhere. PCSO called in their S&R people and the Boy Scouts, and everyone was given an area to search. They were to pay attention to animal activity and smells. I stayed in the motor home and was continually called every time someone smelled a dead animal or saw a rolled up plastic sheet or carpet. I ended up spending three days out in the field, but we never found the lady's body.

The case was difficult from the start. I had hostile witnesses within the family, and there were children who were present when the shooting occurred, but they were being hidden by family members. No one wanted to talk to the cops or help in any way. Nelson was eventually convicted of second degree murder.

I cleared more than one case by simply waiting for the suspect to die. This saved me investigative time, and having to get dressed up for court. Of course it didn't hurt to keep getting cases where the elderly suspect had one foot in the casket.

I got called-out early one morning to a small house located near North Defiance Street and North Park Way. A family member had gone to check on his mother and found her brutally beaten to death. The woman's invalid husband was also missing. The husband was quite elderly, and it was reported that he couldn't walk more than a few feet. He was also constantly hooked up to an oxygen tank. The dead woman was lying in bed and was covered with a bedspread. The bed, floor and walls were painted in sprayed blood. When the spread was pulled back, I found the victim had been hit numerous times. The murder weapon was a solid metal pole about two inches thick and five feet long. It probably weighed forty-five pounds. It was lying on the floor near the bed. It was later discovered that this was a pry bar that was normally kept in the garage.

Family members were contacted and asked for assistance in finding out what happened to the husband. Due to his medical condition and frailties, he was not suspected of being the killer. He couldn't lift his own dick to pee, how in the hell was he going to swing a forty-five pound steel bar. As we processed and photographed the crime scene, a call was made to dispatch to check with the city transit bus that was on the route near the house. Dispatch also called the local cab companies to see if they had picked up anyone near the house. A short time later dispatch called back and reported that Yellow Cab had picked up an elderly man with an oxygen tank on the corner next to the house and had driven him to the Greyhound bus terminal in downtown Tacoma. Greyhound was called and they remembered selling a ticket to the old guy. He caught a bus ride to Chehalis, Washington about sixty miles south of Tacoma down I-5. TPD then received a phone call from a shirttail relative of our victim, who lived east of Chehalis near the town of Morton. The caller was reporting that our missing husband and now suspect, was in a motel in Chehalis and he wanted someone to come and pick him up and drive him to a relative's house.

I jumped into my car and Sgt. Parkhurst climbed into the passenger seat. I lit up the lights and started for Chehalis. Fewer than forty-five minutes later, I pulled into the parking lot of the motel located at the off ramp of I-5 and State Highway 6. We entered the office and found the manager who informed us that our suspect was checked in and staying in room number 2. Parky and I walked down from the office and looked in the window of the room. There sat our killer, watching TV and sucking on his oxygen bottle. The door was open, so we walked in and arrested him without incident. We loaded him and his oxygen tank into the car and drove him back to Tacoma. We debated sending him to the hospital first, as he looked just about as dead as his wife. He was advised of his rights and readily admitted to killing his spouse. He said, "She just would not shut up."

We still couldn't believe that this frail old man who could barely move around, had hefted that big old steel pole and whacked his wife to death. Again luck was on my side, before we could bring him to trial, he died in jail.

NIGHTMARES

I never had a problem dealing with homicide victims; once they were deceased, they just became meat. I would go to autopsies and watch as the coroner turned the body into a canoe. It bothered me a bit when that nasty old bone saw started smoking as the top of the skull was being cut off. Sometimes, I couldn't even finish my sandwich!

Kids were different. I hated going to their autopsies and avoided it like the plague. I would bribe anyone and everyone to go in my place. I had two child cases in a short span of time and both of them have stuck with me all of these years. I still think of them continually.

On December 20, 1983, I was sent on a call to Calvary Cemetery, which was located between 70th and 74th Streets and fronted by Lakewood Drive West. The caller had informed TPD that the maintenance crew had found the body of a small child around 10 a.m. The child was hidden under the boughs of a fir tree in the northeast side of the cemetery. Two part-time ground maintenance workers were trimming fir trees and had just moved to a sixty foot tree. It started snowing heavily, and they climbed under the tree to get out of the weather. They spotted a mound covered with fir needles and one of the two remarked it looked like a body. The other brushed some of the needles away and discovered the child's body. They said they weren't there for more than three seconds and ran for help.

I drove out to the location and was met by a patrolman who was the first officer on the scene. We walked carefully into the tree line and I knelt down to peer under the overhanging limbs. Lying on her back and clothed in a beautiful dress was a child of approximately two years of age. Further inspection showed she had no undergarments on. I thought I was dealing with a possible homicide as the result of a sex crime. I already hated this case. I hated that it's a small little girl who has died, and I hated the son of a bitch who did this to her. I hated myself because, as the lead investigator at this point, I would have to attend the autopsy. Life sucked right then.

It was getting toward late evening and the crime scene needed to be preserved until we could go through it with a fine tooth comb. The little girl was bagged by the coroner and hauled away for the autopsy that would be performed the next day. I had patrolmen assigned to the cemetery to stand guard all night and preserve the area for evidence. I would be back out at first light to start the search.

The next morning I arrived back at Calvary Cemetery and started a grid search of the entire area. I began about 100 feet out and began working my way up to the tree. Hopefully, if the asshole responsible left anything, I would find it. I got a call from Sgt. Parky who told me that if I wanted to continue with the search, he would attend the autopsy and let me know what was found.
"Bless you Parky!" I owed him big time!"

A couple of hours later I had worked my way to the tree and was crawling around on my hands and knees looking for anything. My radio went off and I heard Parky repeating my call sign: "David 17, David 17." I responded back to him, and he told me to find a phone and call him right away. He then gave me the number of the coroner's office. I went up to the cemetery office and used their phone to call Parky.

My first question for him was, “What were the results of the autopsy?” He said, “That’s the reason for the phone call. I didn’t want this information out over the airwaves. The little girl had already been autopsied and they just found out her name. She had been interred at Calvary Cemetery just a couple of days prior. I’ll be right out and we’ll see if we can find out what is going on.”

I found the funeral director and told him we had a situation. I needed to know where the little girl was buried, and we would have to find out what was in the grave, if anything. He checked his records and they showed that the child had been placed in a wall niche in the mausoleum. Parkhurst showed up and the three of us proceeded to the mausoleum. At eye level was the niche with a temporary name plaque. After the remains were placed in the niche a plastic cover was affixed over the entry just using a mild adhesive. Within days, a permanent stone with the child’s information would have been cemented into place. The director started forward to remove it, but I told him not to touch it. We wanted to preserve any possible evidence and fingerprints. I called the crime scene techs to respond and waited for their arrival. When they showed up, we had the plastic face plate dusted for prints after everything had been photographed. Nothing was found so we opened the vault. This space contained the small coffin that our victim had been buried in. This was photographed and again everything was checked for prints. The tiny casket was then removed and opened. Empty! The director was now having visions of major trouble. He had to call the grieving parents and tell them the news. I had to figure out who stole the child's body from the mausoleum, and look for a possible motive.

Over the next couple of weeks I worked this case nonstop trying to come up with a suspect. I had learned that the baby girl had been buried wearing underpants beneath her dress and these were missing. It became obvious that someone had taken the child, removed her clothing, and possibly performed some indignities. There was no evidence of sexual assault, but that still left a whole range of other things that could have been done. I called the FBI to check their databases, and sent teletypes to all law enforcement looking for similar crimes. No luck anywhere. I had reached a dead end! I had no evidence, I had no suspects, and other than "moving/concealing a dead body", I didn't have much in the way of a crime. Then I got the break I wanted and needed.

Parky informed me that they did a survey of the crime scene to pinpoint where everything was should that become an issue in court. The place where the child was found was inside the city limits of Tacoma. The crime scene, which would be the mausoleum, was in Pierce County. The Sheriff now had to assume the case, and it was off my case load. No one was ever arrested for the crime, and the family sued the cemetery and won a large settlement. I still have dreams of the little girl lying beneath the tree on the cold damp ground. God bless the child, and god damn the asshole who put her there.

Another case that resides in my thoughts and dreams was the murder of a little girl by her babysitter. I got the call to a house where a three-year-old child was found not breathing by the fire department paramedics. They were suspicious and wanted detectives to look at the scene. When I arrived, I was shown to a back bedroom where the baby was lying on her back on the bed. A paramedic informed me that when they arrived, they were told by the babysitter… an eighteen year old male… that the baby had choked on baloney. He claimed that he did the Heimlich maneuver on the little girl, but could not get her to expel the chunk of meat in her throat. When she quit breathing, he called the fire department for help.

I walked into the living room and found the babysitter and two other young males sitting and watching television. I separated them and interviewed each one in turn. The two young males claimed they knew nothing and were nowhere near the child. The babysitter stuck to his story, claiming he was watching the girl and gave her baloney for lunch. When she began choking, he tried to help her.

The coroner's office picked up the body, and I prepared to take the babysitter to the station for a formal interview and a statement. As the coroner was leaving, I asked him to do a fast look at the baby girl and call me with what he found. I had the crime scene techs do their thing with photos and evidence collection. I made sure to tell them to place all pieces of baloney they could find, into evidence. I arrived at the station and took the babysitter into the homicide interview room. I questioned him for a couple of hours, but his story remained the same. The little girl was eating baloney and started to choke, so he did the Heimlich on her to no effect. He called for help.

I stepped out of the room and called the coroner's office. They informed me that there was a piece of baloney stuck in the victim's throat, but it didn't appear to have lodged there. The coroner also noted bruising on the stomach of the child. He said it appeared as if the child was struck several times in the abdomen. From the discussion with the coroner and a review of the evidence it appeared to me that the babysitter may have beaten the child then stuck the baloney down the child's throat. I called the coroner one more time and asked if they could do a quick entry on the victim's stomach to see what the extent of the injuries were. They agreed and I went back to the interview room to see if I could get a confession. I stayed on track with my suspect and informed him I knew he had killed the little girl. I pointed out all the inconsistencies and told him I had proof he had beaten the baby and then stuck the baloney down her throat. He kept denying the allegations and told me, "Prove it."

I got called out of the interview room to the phone and again found myself talking to the coroner. He stated that they had opened up the child and found a ruptured intestine, or in other terms, a perforated bowel. This caused severe inflammation from the leakage. The child had more than one rupture and he was guessing the victim may have been struck or punched more than once. He determined this contributed to her death, but he wouldn't document that the child had been murdered. He speculated that the child had been struck in the stomach area which caused peritonitis and pain. The child would have been in distress and crying excessively. At some point, the baloney was crammed in her throat, and she may have suffocated.

I thought I had enough to book the asshole for murder, and did so. The next day I contacted the prosecuting attorney's office to get guidance and arrange the case. I was told they were going to allow the suspect to be released pending the full autopsy report, and that I needed a doctor to go on record that the injuries could only have come from a beating, and not from the Heimlich maneuver.

I spent the next two weeks interviewing every doctor who would talk to me. I could never find one that would go on record or be willing to testify that the child died from the result of homicidal violence. I purchased baloney and had the crime lab try to determine how long it was in the child's throat, or if the piece that was recovered had any teeth marks on it. The lab came back with the finding that no teeth marks were found, and that they could not tell how long the baloney was in her windpipe.

More pressing cases came along and this case was assigned to a female investigator for follow-up. It never went anywhere and was eventually closed as accidental. During this case, for inspiration, I stuck a piece of baloney to the ceiling above my desk. Two years later when we moved from the office, it was still hanging there, and it looked exactly like the day I put it there. I still have nightmares about that child, and I haven't eaten baloney since that case started. What I needed was some comic relief.

We had a detective, Ronny, who was assigned primarily to sex crimes. He was a fatherly-type who could talk to the victims and get their story, and cajole the suspects into confessing. Ron was very trusting. He was also ripe for picking.

During these times of the dinosaur, all reports were handwritten or typed by the detective. The volumes of paper were placed into three-ring binders, and this became the "book." Sometimes there were multiple books based on the extent of the crime, reports, interviews and evidence. Every report or piece of paper placed in the book first had to make its way to the three-hole punch. I started accumulating mounds of the tiny little paper circles that were left over from the punch. Ron always wore a hat and a rain coat. He also carried an umbrella with him constantly. In Tacoma it rained. It rained a lot. The local saying was, "If you can't see Mount Rainier it's raining. If you can see Mount Rainier it is going to rain." The watchword with Ron was: "Always be prepared."

I got his umbrella when he wasn't looking and opened it up. I then poured about 200 pounds of little white paper buttons into it, and then closed it back up. Quitting time came and there was a steady drizzle. Ron headed for the back door, and a bunch of us headed for the nearest window. Ron got outside, looked up, and popped the umbrella open. He was standing there covered in confetti and had a look of pure perplexity on his face. To the best of my recollection, this same gag was pulled on him about twenty times, and it was always met with the same look of astonishment. Ron would spend four days opening his umbrella every day to check for white punches, on the fifth day he would walk outside and Poof! It snowed paper.

Ron had a partner who spent a considerable amount of time peering through binoculars at the girls who walked up and down Tacoma Ave in front of the court house. I decided to do something about this; why should he have all the fun? I walked up to the crime lab office and helped myself to fingerprint powder. This powder is black; very fine graphite and sticks to everything. I then went back to the Crimes Against Persons office, and waited for the detective to leave for a while.

He finally departed with a newspaper for the "Detective Reading Room." I grabbed his binoculars and after wetting my finger and running it around the eyepiece, I dunked it in the fingerprint powder. I then placed the field glasses back on the window sill.

About an hour later, the main door opened and a lady walked in with her teenage daughter. She told the secretary that she needed to report a sex crime that involved her child. The secretary buzzed the detective and informed him that his presence was required for an interview. The next thing we all heard was a screech from the victim and her mother, and a lot of laughing from the secretary. We all poured out into the reception area and there stood our hapless sex crimes detective looking a lot like a raccoon. He had two, black circles ringing his eyes, and had no clue what everyone was laughing and pointing at. Another detective had to take over the interview, as the victim and her mother couldn't put their trust in someone who looked like "Rocky."

"Hey Bobby! Let's put him in the trunk of our police car and give him a ride to Point Defiance."

It did cure his voyeurism, for about a week.

GREEN RIVER

In 1982, the dead bodies of prostitutes began showing up. The first one was found dumped in the Green River south of Seattle. Thus, began a twenty year killing spree that included at least forty-nine victims. It was believed at the time that one person was responsible for all the killings. He was quickly dubbed the Green River Killer. It wouldn't be until 2003 that Gary Ridgway would be convicted of the killings. He has claimed that he murdered as many as seventy women with ties to prostitution.

In 1984 I was contacted by Glade Austin of the Lewis County Sheriff's office. Glade was also a homicide detective and had recently been given a case involving a dead prostitute. A woman's body was found on the bank of the Chehalis River on August 12, 1984. This was near the city of Chehalis about sixty miles south of Tacoma. Detective Austin quickly was able to establish that the female was Monica Anderson, who was linked to the prostitution life style. Anderson lived and worked her trade in Tacoma and was reported as a missing person. Glade contacted me and we spent weeks combing the city for anyone who could shed some light on Anderson's possible disappearance and death. Other prostitutes and Anderson's pimp were all questioned. The two of us sat for endless nights in downtown Tacoma looking for possible suspects. We talked to everyone who knew her, and those who lived in the same apartment building at 9th and Fawcett. The only information we were able to document was that Anderson was last seen alive getting into a brown van in downtown Tacoma on January 24, 1984.

Austin and I went to what was then the secret location of the Green River Task Force. This was a multi-agency group charged with collating all of the dump sites and information coming in regarding the Green River Killer. We spent a couple of days with the group going over all the information they had that might point us in the right direction. We left with nothing that would help identify the killer. Austin spent the better part of a month with me in Tacoma, but eventually had to return to Chehalis. The task force visited the site in Lewis County, and they all believed that their killer was the same one who was responsible for Anderson. This case is still unsolved. All the cases I dealt with where there was an identified suspect and an arrest are gone from my memory. All the cases which were dead ends or the suspect could not be identified, still linger in my thoughts.

“Lazares! I need you to respond to North 50th off of Pearl. Family members can’t find their mother, but they suspect foul play.” Lieutenant Gilmore then handed me a scribbled address and shoved me out of the door. I went to the address and found the family in the back yard. This seemed strange, but what do I know? Then I found out why. The missing lady was a hoarder. The entire house was crammed full of newspapers and magazines. The back door was the only way into the house. To the right was a kitchen, but it was almost unrecognizable as such. Part of the stove and some counter space were visible, but nothing else. To the left was another room, but I had no idea what it was used for. It was full. Then the smell hit me.

This was the smell of death. Once you have been around it, you never mistake it for anything else. There was the underlying smell of decay and garbage from all the crap stuffed into this small house, but there was no denying the sickly-sweet smell of a body that has lain around for a while.

Now I had to find the victim and figure out what in the hell had happened.

This small house was about a thousand square feet. The only way I could search was to start climbing the pile of trash in front of me. It was hot in there, and by the time I reached the top of the pile, I was "sweating like a fat chick at an all you can eat buffet." I was near the ceiling and had about two feet of space to move around in. I had to crawl around on my belly with my head bonking the ceiling. I made a beeline across the crap and entered a hallway. The bathroom was straight ahead and there were bedrooms to my right and left. Both of the bedrooms were completely filled and the bathroom was partially filled. There was just enough room in there to use the toilet. I couldn't see anyone, so I back tracked into what was the living room. I could see the top of the front door and headed in that direction.

Now the smell got really intense. Right in front of the door was what resembled a small avalanche where newspapers and magazines had slid forward. At the bottom of the pile near the floor was the body of our missing lady. Her feet were in the air and her head was down. I could tell by the putrefaction of the body that I wouldn't need to check for a pulse.

I had to figure how the hell I was going to go about processing this as a possible crime scene. I crawled back along the ceiling and slid down the pile to the back door. I informed the family that mom wouldn't be making it to Thanksgiving dinner this year. I then made an executive decision and sent the coroner's men in to retrieve the body. I was willing to bet that our victim died of positional asphyxiation. People get themselves into a position where they cannot breathe properly and they die. I would let the coroner take the victim and do the autopsy while I locked up the house and stationed a patrol unit to guard the place. The next day I was proved right, and released the house to the family. When I left them in the backyard, they were looking for a book of matches.

One Friday morning, I got called-out of the station on an early morning report of a possible homicide. I responded out to 56th and Alder and met the patrol unit in front of an old, two-story house. I was informed that a co-tenant who lived upstairs had found his downstairs tenant dead. To the right of the living room was a nude, young woman lying on the bed. There was a single gunshot wound between her breasts. On the floor was a Remington .41 caliber revolver. Women almost never shoot themselves, but this might be the antithesis.

Another detective arrived to assist me, and we started doing a search of the body and the room. The bullet wound looked to enter our victim's chest straight on, but the exit wound was slightly higher on her back. Based on the position of the body and the path of the wound, we started searching for the expended bullet. I found a hole in the wall near a doorway frame, and marked this location for the evidence technicians to check. This spot would later prove to be where the bullet ended up.

The victim's hands were bagged so that they could be checked for gun powder residue. The body was removed from the house by the coroner's office and an autopsy was performed the following day. The coroner ruled the death as a suicide after paraffin tests showed evidence that the victim had recently fired a gun. That evidence along with the diagram showing the path of the bullet and the hole in the wall convinced everyone that it was not murder. No matter what anyone tried to tell the girl's parents, they could never accept the ruling and continually called the police department demanding further investigations.

WORKING FOR UNCLE SUGAR

By using my position and rank in the Army, I was able to attend somewhere in the neighborhood of twenty-eight schools. I was still working for Tacoma P.D, but was also doing my time in the Army Reserve. I went to two Officer Survival Instructor's courses and three schools for Dignitary Protection. I was trained by the U.S. Law Enforcement community and by L.A. Police instructors. I became an FBI-trained Hostage Negotiator.

I also got to attend the training course that became the most fun I've ever had with my clothes on. In 1982, I was sent to the Terrorism and Counterterrorism Driving Course put on by the Feds at Summit Point Race Track. This road course was in Jefferson County, West Virginia which was two hours west of Washington, D.C.

This driving course started with me and my fellow students learning how to crash cars into other cars, in case there was a road block we needed to escape. I got to smash through two or three cars set-up to make you stop. The instructors would tow or push cars onto the roadway, and I would have to crash through them. I can't remember how many vehicles had to be towed away, but they filled a small lot. I was also taught the Pursuit Immobilization Technique or PIT maneuver. Then I learned to do J-turns and Bootleg turns. When not doing the turns, I was out on the track learning high speed driving. I was taught all the moves that a race car driver learns in his career. I was running the same course a Formula One race car would use and going into and out of turns and corners, only I was doing it in a Ford Crown Vic at 100 miles an hour. I was loving it!

The Bootleg turn was accomplished by pulling on the parking brake or stepping on the brake pedal. When the tires locked up I would spin the steering wheel hard left. This maneuver would cause the car to spin 180 degrees extremely fast, and by releasing the brake, I could accelerate away from the danger. This turn was originated by Junior Johnson when he was running moonshine from his father's still. Junior went on to become a famous NASCAR racer.

The J-turn was accomplished by first slamming on the brakes to stop the forward momentum of the car, then shifting into reverse and begin rapidly backing up. The steering wheel was quickly spun while also stepping on the brake pedal and shifting into neutral. The car would spin 180 degrees, and as the nose came around I would shift into drive and accelerate away. This stuff was fun.

The PIT maneuver was done by placing my vehicle's front tires on a line with the pursued car's rear tires. Then I would edge in and make contact. Once contact was made with the other car, I would turn into that car sharply and push. This would cause the pursued car to spin out. The correct action to take if you were the recipient of the PIT, was a J-turn to drive out of the spin. This was another maneuver honed to perfection on the early NASCAR tracks.

All day and part of the night was spent doing these maneuvers over and over. Finally, it was graduation day, or more to the point, graduation night. As soon as it got dark, each student would head out onto the road course that wound around through the trees for two miles. During the trip around the track, I would be attacked at some point by the driving instructors. This usually began with a road block. It would be my job to perform a Bootleg or J-turn when it was necessary and then flee. The instructors would do everything they could to spin you out or stop you using the PIT maneuver. You had to make it safely around the two mile track to graduate. I passed and graduated. Some had to remain and take portions of the course over again. If I had been thinking clearly, I would still be there trying to pass that course.

I had been doing protective service assignments since 1978. Or as I called it: "Bullet Catching 101." If someone tried to shoot, stab or blow up my protectee, I was expected to throw my body in front of the threat. Ha!

Based on my talents to drive fast and crazy, I ended up being the chase car driver on most missions. In a convoy with a dignitary, there would be at least the Primary's Car and the Chase Car. The primary car would contain the driver and a Close Proximity agent and the protectee in the rear seat. The job of the chase car was to bust any roadblocks, or failing that, the chase crew would pull in front of the primary car and engage the attackers with lethal and overwhelming force. In the chase car there were usually at least two protective staff and they would be packing personal weapons, shotguns, and an automatic MP-5 or Uzi. The primary car would drive fast and the chase car would drive right on their rear bumper. The driver of the chase car had better have lighting fast reflexes or you would be buying the beer. If for some reason you banged into the back end of the primary car; drinks were on you. I never had to buy. Now I was a "school trained" fast and crazy driver. Not just self-taught.

I had a lot of interesting assignments over the years. One of my first trips involved Deng Xiaoping, who was then the 1st Vice Premier of Communist China. I spent a month in 1979 travelling with him all over the U.S. providing protection. We had three teams and we kept leap frogging from city to city. One team would be with Deng, and the other two teams would move to other cities and prepare for his arrival. His own personal security officers were travelling with him but were not allowed to carry weapons in the U.S.

During this trip, I was instrumental in thwarting an attack on the Premier by a crazed penguin at Sea World in San Diego, and I personally threw my body in front of a killer whale whose intentions are still not clear. For these brave actions, I was allowed to get drunk with the Chinese security guys when we were in San Francisco, and I got to meet a movie star.

We had been invited to a behind the scene tour of Sea World and I escorted the Premier into the penguin enclosure. I found myself walking on ice, surrounded by penguins, and slipping and sliding in penguin shit. I was wearing a three piece suit and leather soled shoes. What could possibly go wrong? A giant penguin decided that his mission in life at that particular moment was to bite the Premier in the right rear butt cheek. I immediately assumed it was a Taiwanese penguin, who was a mainland hating anti-communist. I tried to draw my service weapon but began sliding. The Premier wasn't too keen on getting his ass bit, and while trying to get away, also began sliding. I grabbed the Premier and held him up while zoo staff tackled the penguin. Had I been quicker with my gun I would have assured myself a place in the "Protective Detail Hall of Fame."

We cleaned all the attached penguin shit from our shoes and proceeded to the killer whale pool. I escorted the Premier down to the ledge next to the pool and stood behind him.

The whale trainer blew a whistle, and the next thing I knew "Shamu" was sliding up onto the ledge with my protectee.

"Oh shit! I never should have left the machine gun in the trunk of the car."

The whale trainer assured me all was fine and if we wanted to we could pet "Shamu."

I thought that was a splendid idea because the closest I had ever gotten to a whale was a blind date in 9th grade.

"Old Deng" said he would pass on the petting unless they were serving the whale for dinner.

We packed up and moved from San Diego north to San Francisco.

The Chinese Consulate in San Francisco hosted a dinner party with cocktails. The Asian security guys were always trying to get the U.S. guys drunk, so someone was always assigned the duty of drinking with them. First your team mates would take your gun away from you and they would relieve you of your badge and ID. No one on the U.S team wanted an international incident. That night was my night as the duty drunk.

The Chinese would bring water glasses full of Mao Tai, which is liquor made from distilled Sorghum. It is 144 proof and has the distinctive flavor of lighter fluid with a barnyard or cabbage smell. If you could get one down, you could drink Mao Tai all night long or until you were rendered unconscious. I later learned that the Chinese security guys would have Mao Tai in their glass for the first toast, but after that only water. The whole intent was to get the Americans drunk.

On this night, the Mao Tai worked its magic on me. I was on my third toast of the evening having learned that "Gam Bai" means "empty glasses" or bottoms up. When, who should walk up to me for an introduction, but Shirley Temple? Or I cornered her. The story differs depending on who is telling it. In my telling, Shirley said, "Oh Michael! You are the hero who single-handedly fought an emperor penguin to the death and saved the Vice Premier!" She then handed me her name tag, which she autographed.

Then there is the story being bandied about by unreliable, lying Special Agents. In their version, I walked up to Shirley Temple Black and proclaimed, "It's Shirley Temple!" I then yanked her name tag off of her left bosom which may or may not be the real one (bosom, not name tag!) I was then carried bodily to the garden outside and told to stay there until it was safe to return to the party."

A few minutes later, Ms. Temple walked to the garden area and confronted me. She said, "As long as you have my name tag, I might as well autograph it for you!" It was signed with a flourish and a wink. I kept this memento safe until I got to New York a week later and lost it. I still think the maid stole it.

I spent a lot of time in Washington, D.C., usually two weeks at a time. This was the 80's and I was chase car driver for the Secretary of Defense, Caspar Weinberger. This was always a thrill a moment followed by hours of unrelenting boredom. His team would pick him up at his house at 5 a.m. and rush balls to the wall for the White House. He would get dropped-off for his morning meeting with the President while we waited and waited. Then out he would come, and it was another mad dash for the Pentagon. He would head in for his daily regimen of meeting after meeting while we sat in an office down the hall from his domain. And sat and sat.

I always hoped that during the day, he would get a summons somewhere just to break the boredom. Maybe we can get some dumb country to declare war with the U.S. At least we would get catered meals in the "War Room."

This is how glamorous the days were. Up at 3 or 4 a.m. to get ready and stage at Weinberger's house. Then all day driving or sitting, and never being off-duty because we never knew when we might have to go somewhere. There were planned trips, and then someone would throw a small crisis into the mix and we had to go to some unplanned meeting. Finally, at 5 or 6 p.m., we took him home where he got a nap and then changed into his party clothes. Meanwhile, the cars had to be gassed and plans had to be made for another movement at 8 p.m. to a private home, or the White House, or some country's Embassy for cocktails and dinner. This meant I could count on eating a cold sandwich on the hood of my car and not getting to bed until midnight. Then I got to get up and do it all over again the next day. Fourteen days in D.C. meant a lot of eighteen to twenty hour days, and maybe one day off if Weinberger stayed home on Sunday.

Since I was close to the west coast, I was also a frequent flyer to the Bay Area. San Francisco was Weinberger's home and he often visited there. Every time we went there he would try and ditch us so he could visit with friends or family without us around. His driver always snitched on him to us about his plans and we would follow him discretely and hide down the street.

There were other missions to other places, and some of these were downright fun. One trip was with the Secretary of Defense for Nigeria. He was supposed to visit Nellis Air Force Base outside of Las Vegas, to see jets up close and to watch the fighters engage in mock dogfights. What happened was he landed, and his aide walked up to me and said, "The Minister has seen jets before. What he wants to do is go downtown and see naked blondes."

"Well OK then. I'll gas up the car and get a fistful of one dollar bills."

And that is what we did for three days. We went to every pole dancer and strip show in Vegas where the minister got to drop a lot of money supplied by Uncle Sam.

When the mission came to an end, we were checking the rooms at Nellis that the Minister's staff stayed in. They cleaned-out every room of toilet paper; towels and ashtrays, and of course the mini-bars. We lined up their luggage on the tarmac and confiscated all of the mini-bottles of booze. This was about $100 of alcohol per room. The air force charged them for the items, but somehow the little bottles never made it back. We, on the other hand, had one hell of a "Wheels-up Party" to show our appreciation for the Nigerians. After spending days planning a protection detail, and doing all the site surveys and running routes, we were burned out. Then the actual detail would begin and that meant many more long hours. Finally, we would escort the protectee to the airport and put him on a plane to his next destination. As soon as the plane left the ground (wheels up), the party would start.

Then there was the famous trip to El Salvador with Colin Powell, who at the time was Chairman of the Joint Chiefs. Another agent, named Kevin, and I were sent down to El Salvador a few days before Powell was to arrive, so we could do a total inspection of the capital, San Salvador, and several sites out in the country. Powell was going to spend three days in country inspecting the military.

Kevin and I were picked up at the airport by the U.S. Embassy in a Chevrolet Suburban that was so heavily armored plated it couldn't get out of its own way. We were situated in the rear seat, and behind us in the cargo area was a guy armed with a machine gun. He sat facing backward and had both rear doors open. To my left and my right in the back seat were two more guys sitting in swivel chairs and also armed with machine guns. And finally there was one more machine-gun toting guard sitting in the right front seat.

When we moved, no one, especially someone on a motorcycle, was allowed to get next to us. The favorite trick of the bad guys was to pull alongside your car and either shoot you or plant a bomb on top of your roof. Or they would wait at a traffic light and then assassinate you. When we stopped for any reason, the doors would all open up, and the guards would dismount and take up firing positions around the car. As I was being driven to the embassy, I noticed that every single business had a guard standing out front carrying an AK-47.

"Holy shit! I've gone to sleep in Central America and woken up in Detroit."

At the embassy, I was told that under no circumstances was I to leave the hotel without calling and getting an armed escort. I had two choices as to where to stay. Would I like to stay in the hotel that is owned by the narco-terrorists of South America, or the hotel owned by the mafia from the U.S.? I'll take the good old USA. I'm also beginning to think I know why they sent us down here to keep Powell safe. This is one dangerous country.

I checked into the hotel and got unpacked, and then called Kevin to see if he wanted a beer before we had to get started with the route surveys. We needed to visit all the places Chairman Powell would visit, and we had to map out the routes, and locate danger points and suspected ambush locations. That could wait until the next day. When we got to the bar we found that they were hosting a "Fiesta" for the guests. We grabbed beers and got in line. They had everything imaginable to eat and it all looked delicious. We pigged out!

About 3 a.m., I was struck with what can only be described as "The Shits." I was no sooner seated than I had to unseat to puke. I finally resolved this issue by sitting to shit and holding the waste basket to vomit. I became so dehydrated that I had to crawl out to a vending machine in the hall and get as much 7-up as I could. I sat all night on the toilet and poured the pop in only to hear it splash out my other end.

By morning, I was dead or near death. I didn't care what the embassy said, I needed help. I got my gun and all the ammo I could carry and walked doubled-over out of the hotel and down the street to the Mercado (market). I was holding my stomach with one hand and clamping my butt cheeks together with the other one, trying not to leak. I found the Pharmacia (pharmacy) and was trying to make myself understood, but the people working there only spoke Spanish. I was desperate! I couldn't wait another second or I'd be buying diapers too! Then I spotted a familiar pink bottle sitting on a shelf behind the counter. I crawled over the countertop and headed for the Pepto with three people chasing me. As I grabbed it, all of them immediately started nodding their heads and saying "Si!"

I snatched another large bottle and gave them a wad of cash as I chugged about half a bottle before heading back to the hotel. As soon as I got back to my room, I felt the dreaded cramps and scooted back to the bathroom. I was now drinking Pepto-Bismol and it no sooner passed my lips than it was showing up pink in the bottom of the toilet bowl. It didn’t even slow down.

Kevin called, he was equally afflicted and down for the count. We called the embassy and begged-off on the day's sightseeing. I was dying. I pulled the TV down the hall as far as the cord would reach and now I could sit on the toilet and watch sitcoms while pouring Pepto and 7-up in.

That night, I was still sitting enjoying my pink cocktails when I heard a “pop-pop-pop”, and I could see tracers arching up past my bedroom window. My first thought was I hadn’t left enough cash at the Pharmacia. Then there was a large explosion and all of the lights went out. It wasn’t like I had to see, to do what I was doing. A couple of hours later the lights came back on, and the next day I found out the rebels had blown up another power station.

Two days later, Powell showed up, but Kevin and I were still battling the Hershey squirts. There was no one else to cover Powell so we had to go. We had finally got the route recon done and the site inspections, but they were not as complete as they should have been.

We convoyed out to the military headquarters, where Powell was to do an inspection of the troops and then give a speech. I was located on one side of the parade ground and Kevin was across from me. Powell was located in the middle and he was facing toward the main building where the bathrooms were located. I was standing there in my suit with a radio bug in my ear and a transmitter down my sleeve, and hanging out my cuff. Then it hit!

I talked into my wrist, “Kevin! You watch him!”
Then I sprinted across the field toward the toilet holding my ass cheeks in an iron grip. I looked at Powell and he was staring at me. I couldn’t imagine what was going through his mind. Then I heard Kevin yelling on the radio for me to hurry. He wasn’t sure he could wait another second.

My visit only took about two seconds and there was nothing to wipe. I had just needed a quick blot and I was done. I yanked-up my pants and raced back. As I was sprinting back to my post, I spotted Kevin heading to where I had just been. I stole a look at Powell, and he was speechless, watching Kevin sprinting across the parade field. Then I think it dawned on him. There was a moment of enlightenment on his face and then a smile.

Somehow we survived the trip and I did several more with Colin Powell, even returning to El Salvador for another visit. I packed all of my own food with me though. Powell always looked at me a little strangely after that first trip. After the trip to El Salvador, I went back to D.C. I had to go to Walter Reed Army Hospital and give specimens for about a week. They kept trying different tests and antibiotics, but it took a month for the "El Salvador two-step" to finally disappear.

I was called by the Port of Seattle Police Department one day at the P.D. The 1990 Goodwill Games were coming to Seattle, and they were being tasked to provide motorcades and close proximity protection to visiting dignitaries. However, they had never been trained to do any of that. I was hired to prepare classes and teach them all they needed to know, including anti-terrorist driving. I ended up spending a week teaching them. After I did the classroom work, we did practical exercises all over Sea-Tac Airport. We did motorcades into and out of the airport property and had simulated missions to some of the Game's venues. Then I got to spend two days on one of the runways teaching all of the trick driving techniques I had learned at Summit Raceway. It was a lot of fun, but the Port of Seattle got a wee bit upset because we damaged about three police cars. I think the total was: one engine, one transmission, four or five ruined tires, and a smashed bumper.

There was a young and upcoming country singer by the name of Mindy McCready. At the time, she was barely 17 years old and on the path to stardom. She was living in Florida and maybe heading for Nashville. Two cops from Florida were acting as her bodyguards, but had no training in doing "close personal protection." They called me!

They used their contacts and got in touch with the FBI who knew of my work. It was a nice referral, and was looking like it would morph into a job with McCready. However, like most things of this nature when you start explaining all that was involved to a couple of cops, they start thinking you will screw them out of the good thing they got going. They finally decided that they would learn on their own and just wing it. McCready went to Nashville, and the two cops got bumped to the curb as soon as the record producers and managers came on board and learned how inept the two were. Of course, McCready became a handful for her watchers and handlers. She had her troubles with alcohol and mental health issues, and would eventually die of a self inflicted gunshot wound.

In 1991, I got called to a secret meeting with the FBI who were controlling a Russian mobster residing in the U.S. The plan that was hatched called for me to set up a school somewhere locally, and then train Russians in anti-terrorist driving and close proximity protection. The FBI wanted to be able to monitor the students who would be coming for the schooling. The Russian mob had penetrated, and for the most part, taken over the banking industry in their homeland. The bankers were being shot and kidnapped, so they needed protection. I was asked to train the protection agents.

I spent a lot of time getting the school set up on paper and arranging for the use of Seattle International Raceway. The classes and all the driving courses would take place at the race track. Before I could get a commitment from the Russians, the local mobster did what all crooks do. He went out and did some more crime. For this, he was arrested and then deported back to Moscow. I was told that when he arrived back in Russia, his fellow mob members took unkindly to the fact that he had screwed-up his assignment, not to mention talking to the FBI. They took him for a ride and shot him dead. Another missed opportunity.

I did a bunch more missions to D.C., but Weinberger was out and Dick Cheney was in. I didn't care for Cheney, and really didn't want to work for him. As soon as I could arrange it, I jumped back to Collin Powell's detail. He was a true gentleman and just a wonderful person to be around. Plus, he was a military man where Weinberger and Cheney were civilians trying their best to screw-up the military.

Again in 1991, I received a call from CBS television wanting to know if I could provide protection to Janine Turner, who was the star of the show "Northern Exposure." The show was filming in a little town in the Cascade Mountains called "Roslyn." I had a small private company at that time which was doing protective details, movements of high value diamond shipments, hotel security consulting, and the odd jobs with law enforcement. This was another referral from the FBI. I called my good friend and co-worker, Richy Moothart, and asked if he wanted to spend a few days covering Janine's butt. He said something to the effect that I didn't even have to pay him.

Roslyn had been formed as a town in 1885, when coal was found there. It became a company town and stayed prosperous until the mines started shutting down in 1920's. Later in life, Roslyn became the stand-in for the fictitious town of Cicely, Alaska, in the show "Northern Exposure."

Turner had begun receiving death threats from an unknown source, and CBS wanted to make sure no harm came to her. Most of the interior shots of the show were done in Redmond, Washington, but on occasion they did some filming outside in Roslyn. When this happened, I would send Richy to drive Turner from her home near Seattle, to Roslyn. He would then stand around all day hoping to get to shoot someone, or at the very least throw himself on Turner. Finally, the issue was resolved when the FBI tracked down the sender of the letters and arrested him. He was just a love struck fan that Turner had ignored.

I would have the opportunity to spend several months in Florida with Norm Schwarzkopf. After "Stormin Norman" kicked a bunch of ass in the Middle East, he ended up with a bounty on his head. A large, protective detail was assigned to guard him, and I was in charge of the surveillance/counter-surveillance detail. I spent every day running around Tampa and Hillsborough County looking for suspicious Arabs, or cars with bombs attached, or suspicious Arabs with bombs attached.

Norm was given a golf membership to the Cheval Country Club, but he didn't play. He was also comped a couple sets of clubs. I took it upon myself to visit the managers of the club and inform them of my duties with Schwarzkopf. I impressed upon them that I needed to travel around the golf course in order to search for undesirables and suspicious persons. In order not to appear out of place and to blend in with the locals, I suggested that I bring golf clubs and use one of their carts.

They thought that it would be even better if I just went ahead and played, and that way no one would suspect that I was conducting counter surveillance. I told them that maybe twice a week would work-out for me, and they said to be sure and not breathe a word to any of the members.

Behind Norm's house we had parked a small, motor home that contained radios, weapons, and two Military Policemen. The motor home sat between Norm's back fence and the golf fairway. They were on a twelve hours on, twelve hours off shift schedule and were bored to tears. I thought to myself that I should make sure they knew I had their best interest at heart and was concerned that they may have gotten tired and dozed off. I began smacking two or three golf balls into the side of their mobile home, whenever I happened to be playing.

"Hey! You can't raise your middle finger at me. Is that gun loaded?"

Norm was another military man who looked-out for his troops, and that included his protection detail. And, like Powell, Schwarzkopf was a gentleman and a pleasure to work for.

END OF THE LINE

We all have a cup. Every little occurrence life hands you put a drop in the cup. When the cup is full, you are done. Everyone's cup is a different size. Some cups hold gallons and never seem to fill. Other cups hold only a small amount and fill-up way too soon.

I spent almost five years in Robbery/Homicide dealing with every kind of violence and mayhem one person could inflict on another. I can't remember a weekend when the phone didn't ring at 2:00 a.m with another request by my supervisor to respond to a dead body, or one that may soon be in that condition. Tacoma had its share of homicides, and aggravated assaults were the norm on any given day. If the assault was serious or might result in a death then I got called out.

Stress was building, but I didn't know it. When I did recognize it, I tended to ignore the symptoms. I had been fighting a losing battle with stress and anger since coming home from Vietnam. I had the candle lit on both ends and

for good measure built a fire in the middle.
As I was fond of saying, “I’m tap dancing as fast as I can.”

I was working fifty or sixty hours a week on cases involving death and mayhem. Then adding to the fun and excitement, and to insure I had no quality time with myself or family, I became an Officer Survival instructor with the police department. Beside my other duties, I was teaching combat pistol and shotgun, and giving classes in unarmed defensive tactics.

I was still in the Army Reserves and was often being called up for missions. I had become an expert in Protective Services and traveled the world providing close proximity protection for U.S Cabinet members, the Department of Defense, and foreign dignitaries. These were always high stress assignments with long hours and no glory. Plus, I was still doing my weekend warrior drills and the two week summer camps. Most of the time, I was doing three or four weekend drills instead of the one, and summer camps were most often a month long.

January 24th, 1985. It was a normal Thursday evening. I had just gotten home from work a couple of hours earlier and the phone rang. I was told that I needed to respond to the 1000 block of North Prospect Street for a multiple homicide. One of the victims was reported to be a police officer. The one call no one wants. Having to deal with a child victim is tough enough, but a fellow officer is devastating. While racing to the scene, I was envisioning every single police officer I knew. At that point, I had no more information, and my mind was really revving up. Was it someone I had worked with or been in the academy with?

When I got to the crime scene, I was told that the police officer was Craig Nollmeyer, and that he died in the street from a bullet wound to his head from a .44 caliber magnum. The suspect ambushed the officers from a hidden spot in the alley. Officers returned fire and the suspect, Kenneth Schrader was hit. He was currently in the hospital being guarded while undergoing surgery.

I was informed that this was a multi-location crime scene. Schrader had attacked his wife, Elaine with a knife and slashed his thirteen year old stepson, Warren, across the scalp. Warren then fled to the next door neighbor, Jill Lyte, to call the police. As Lyte was on the phone to the police, they heard a single shot, which was probably Schrader ending Elaine's life. A few seconds later, Lyte saw Schrader outside her front window. As Lyte was trying to herd Warren, and a friend of hers who was visiting, into a bathroom, Schrader fired twice through the front window. He then kicked in the front door and shot Lyte in the arm. Schrader then calmly walked-out the rear of the home and down the alley.

Police Officer Nollmeyer and his partner William Taylor, had arrived, saw Schrader in the alley, and heard his gun click twice. Nollmeyer called out, "His gun is empty." Then there was a shot, and Nollmeyer fell. Taylor then engaged Schrader in a gun fight and Schrader went down. Two motorcycle officers pulled up and they saw Schrader start to bring his gun up. Officer Jim Smith then shot Schrader again. Schrader was hit a total of four times and survived; later to be arrested.

I had a crime scene in the alley where Schrader ambushed the officers, another scene where Officer Nollmeyer had been shot and killed, and nearby was the patrol car with bullet holes from the gun fight with Schrader. I also had the original homicide scene with Schrader's wife's body and the assault on the stepson. Then, there was the neighbor's home with the assault and wounding of that resident. Thankfully, a lot of help was on the way.

Bill Parkhurst and Gary Wiegand showed up to be the on-site supervisors. Parky took the houses and was directing the accumulation of statements and witnesses. Gary got stuck with the outside scene where Nollmeyer was shot. Detectives arrived eager to assist in any way, and I know I needed it. I would not see my house again for over twenty-four hours.

Schrader would survive his wounds and be convicted of his crimes. He is serving life in prison. My own opinion is that he should never have left that alley alive. The same thoughts occurred to other Tacoma officers when they responded to the murder scene of Officer Larry Frost on September 9, 1977. I have had discussions with fellow officers who made an attempt to get to the shooter and end his life. It is a very real thought in the mind of many policemen when they find a fellow officer and friend lying dead. Officer Frost's killer was found lying naked in an alley. He turned and looked up at, then patrolman Larry Ihlen, and said, I'm a man. Are you a man? I'm Jesus." The courts found him insane at the time and he was committed to the state hospital, but released after a short time.

Police officers won't talk to anyone else about these thoughts, but they share them amongst their brethren. It is not a healthy lifestyle. I always wondered how some guys could just turn all of this off when they left at the end of the day. I guess I never could. Everything I had seen or been exposed to just kept filling my cup until the day I went toward the light.

I had just turned forty years of age and had died.

This is the end
Beautiful friend
This is the end
My only friend, the end
It hurts to set you free
But you'll never follow me
The end of laughter and soft lies
The end of nights we tried to die

This is the end

Lyrics by Jim Morrison
The Doors

About the Author

Michael served two tours of duty in Vietnam as a combat helicopter pilot. He flew in the Army for seven years and was a flight instructor. He remained in the US Army Reserves, and retired after twenty-eight years. While in the USAR, he participated in numerous Protective Service Missions around the world. Michael became a PSM Instructor and trained various law enforcement personnel. He was also an Anti-Terrorism Driving Instructor.

Michael served as an officer in the Tacoma Police Department and retired as a detective in the homicide unit. He spent a total of thirty years in law enforcement and retired from the Division of Fraud for the State of Washington.

He has three children and two grandchildren, and is living in Arizona with his wife Heleen.

See what other books and projects Michael is working on. Visit him at www.mdlazaresauthor.com

Made in the USA
San Bernardino, CA
15 April 2014